THE PRICE OF WATER
Trends in OECD Countries

ORGANISATION FOR ECONOMIC CO-OPERATION AND DEVELOPMENT

ORGANISATION FOR ECONOMIC CO-OPERATION AND DEVELOPMENT

Pursuant to Article 1 of the Convention signed in Paris on 14th December 1960, and which came into force on 30th September 1961, the Organisation for Economic Co-operation and Development (OECD) shall promote policies designed:

- to achieve the highest sustainable economic growth and employment and a rising standard of living in Member countries, while maintaining financial stability, and thus to contribute to the development of the world economy;

- to contribute to sound economic expansion in Member as well as non-member countries in the process of economic development; and

- to contribute to the expansion of world trade on a multilateral, non-discriminatory basis in accordance with international obligations.

The original Member countries of the OECD are Austria, Belgium, Canada, Denmark, France, Germany, Greece, Iceland, Ireland, Italy, Luxembourg, the Netherlands, Norway, Portugal, Spain, Sweden, Switzerland, Turkey, the United Kingdom and the United States. The following countries became Members subsequently through accession at the dates indicated hereafter: Japan (28th April 1964), Finland (28th January 1969), Australia (7th June 1971), New Zealand (29th May 1973), Mexico (18th May 1994), the Czech Republic (21st December 1995), Hungary (7th May 1996), Poland (22nd November 1996) and Korea (12th December 1996). The Commission of the European Communities takes part in the work of the OECD (Article 13 of the OECD Convention).

Publié en français sous le titre :
LE PRIX DE L'EAU
Les tendances dans les pays de l'OCDE

Foreword

In 1987, OECD published *Pricing of Water Services*. This publication reviewed pricing practices in several OECD countries for such water services as public supplies, sewage disposal, and direct abstractions. The study also addressed a few related issues – for example, water subsidies and agricultural irrigation systems. It reviewed how pricing systems for each of these components actually operated in practice (*i.e.* description), and discussed how the environmental and economic efficiency of those systems might be improved (*i.e.* prescription). However, little distinction was drawn at the time among pricing practices in individual economic sectors (*e.g.* households, industry and agriculture).

This report provides an update, and some expansion, of the information contained in the 1987 report. In this respect, it can be interpreted as a type of "10-year progress report" on the recommendations made in that report concerning improved water pricing practices in OECD countries. It summarises new information on current practices and recent trends in water pricing for the household, agricultural and industrial sectors. It also addresses several "non-sectoral" pricing topics, such as water subsidies and institutional changes. Finally, it contains considerably wider coverage of OECD countries than the 1987 report did.

The book can be read in conjunction with the following related publications, all of which were produced under the "Natural Resource Management" Programme of the OECD Environment Policy Committee:

– OECD (1997), *Water Subsidies and the Environment*.

– OECD (1999), *Agricultural Water Pricing in OECD Countries*.

– OECD (1999), *Industrial Water Pricing in OECD Countries*.

– OECD (1999), *Household Water Pricing in OECD Countries*.

Early drafts of these papers were prepared by **Alberto Garrido,** Universidad Politéchnica de Madrid, Spain (agriculture); **William Baker** and **Sophie Tremolet,** NERA Economic Consultants, London, UK (industry); **Paul Herrington,** University of Leicester, UK (households); and **Andreas Kraemer** and **Matthias Buck,** ECOLOGIC

OECD 1999

Consulting, Berlin, Germany (subsidies). All of the papers have also benefited from technical contributions made by an *ad hoc* group of OECD water pricing experts. Each of these contributions is gratefully acknowledged.

The book is published under the responsibility of the Secretary-General of the OECD.

Table of Contents

OECD 1999

List of Boxes

List of Tables

List of Figures

OECD 1999

OECD 1999

Chapter 1

Executive Summary

The objective of this report is to summarise new developments and trends in water pricing practices which have occurred over the last ten years in OECD countries. More specifically, it aims to provide information about:

- water pricing *policies actually in place* in different OECD countries, and "groups" of countries or sectors of the economy where particular practices are most predominant;
- *trends in pricing practices* occurring in various economic sectors, especially the household, agriculture, and industry sectors; and
- *progress being achieved* toward the goal of more efficient, effective, and equitable water pricing practices in the OECD region.

Given the widely differing demands on water supply systems, and the different institutional and cultural frameworks within which pricing policies have to operate, it is not surprising that there continues to be considerable variation in pricing structures across OECD countries. Nevertheless, most countries do appear to have made progress over the past decade toward the goal of more efficient and effective pricing of their water services. The following developments stand out in particular:

- Increasing management autonomy by water utilities, reflecting a shift in the role of governments away from being the "provider", and toward being the "regulator" of water services. While this trend is generally accompanied by an increased role for the private sector, most countries have opted for the "concession" model (whereby the private sector participates in managing some services, but the public sector retains ownership control over the system). The "full privatisation" model (*i.e.* complete private sector ownership) is not widely encountered.
- A general movement away from the pricing of water services solely to generate revenues, and toward the use of tariffs to achieve a wider range of economic, environmental, and social objectives. Awareness also seems to be growing about which particular elements of water price structures (connection charges, volumetric and fixed charges, etc.) can best achieve which particular policy objectives.

– A decline in aggregate industrial water consumption across OECD countries, with some industrial sectors in particular leading the way. These sectors may be more sensitive to changes in water prices, or have a greater range of water-saving technologies at their disposal than others. In the household and agricultural sectors, an aggregate OECD trend is more difficult to discern (*i.e.* consumption in some countries is increasing, while it is decreasing in others).

– A clear trend in the household sector away from decreasing-block and flat-fee pricing structures, and toward uniform volumetric or increasing-block tariff systems. Most countries also now use two-part tariffs (*i.e.* with fixed and volumetric components), with the volumetric portion making up at least 75% of the total water bill.

– A tendency for industrial water users that draw water from the public system (representing 23 per cent of the industrial freshwater used on average in OECD countries, with the rest direct abstractions) to be charged according to the same structure as household users, but with a more frequent use of volumetric pricing.

– A tendency for most agricultural tariff structures to be based on the surface area irrigated, and to be charged either as a flat rate or according to crop type. Volume-based charging systems are the next most common, although a variety of other structures also exist.

– Continuing increases in the penetration of household water metering. Nearly two-thirds of OECD Members already meter more than 90% of single-family houses, and some countries are now expanding their metering of apartments. Industrial water use is already metered in most countries, while agricultural use is metered in only a few.

– The existence of a wide range of practices concerning the use of water taxes and charges in pricing schedules. VAT is the most common tax applied, with rates in some countries exceeding 20%. Some taxes and charges are levied with explicit environmental purposes in mind, and the revenues raised are sometimes also earmarked for specific environmental uses.

– Household water supply and sewage disposal prices have generally increased, and significantly so in a few countries. Of the 19 countries for which enough data was available for this study, all but one exhibited real per annum increases in water supply prices during this period, and five experienced average rates of real price increase of 6% or more per annum.

– The common use of special tariff structures and/or rates for large industrial water users. Occasionally, these special arrangements may cover water quality variables as well as quantity ones.

– An increasing trend of industrial water consumers going "off-system" (*i.e.* to directly abstract water supplies or to recycle and treat their own waste waters before directly discharging them) as these options become more financially viable in the face of increasing charges for publicly supplied water services.

– The continuance of a situation where agricultural water prices remain relatively low compared with household and industry prices, and where a few countries continue to apply no charges at all to irrigation water abstractions.

– The increasing application of abstraction charges (in place in at least 14 OECD countries) or the use of licensing systems to manage direct abstractions by large industrial and agricultural water users.

– An increased tendency to charge for wastewater disposal on the basis of treatment costs actually faced by service providers. For this reason, water charges related to pollution have increased substantially in recent years. There is also a trend in the direction of separating treatment and supply charges on individual water bills – a step which will inevitably encourage more accountability on the part of service providers.

– More acceptance of the need for "full cost recovery" in the provision of water services. This is accompanied by significant reductions in both total subsidies and cross-subsidies between different user groups. Even where subsidies still exist, there is now more emphasis on the need to make these subsidies transparent.

– A growing awareness that subsidising water use is not necessarily the best way to achieve sectoral economic or social goals, and that some economic and social goals are actually harmed in the longer-term by using a subsidy-based approach.

– Further evidence that households, businesses, and agricultural producers generally *do* change their water consumption patterns in response to changes in such variables as price levels, metering penetration, and seasonal pricing.

– Concerns about the affordability of household water services have led to the development of several innovative "social" tariff structures, many of which contribute to environmental and economic goals at the same time.

11

Chapter 2

Introduction

In 1987, the OECD published *Pricing of Water Services* (OECD, 1987a). That report reviewed the pricing practices for piped water services as well as direct uses of the resource (abstractions, discharges) existing in several OECD countries at the time. It also examined practical experiences with a number of related "special" topics, such as metering and the subsidisation of water use. It noted that a wide range of water pricing techniques existed across OECD countries, often because of different resource endowments, but also because of different economic needs, cultural traditions, and development paths. Finally, it emphasised that marginal cost pricing is theoretically the most efficient approach to pricing water services, but found that this approach was seldom being used in practice.

This report is intended to serve as a type of "ten year progress report" to the 1987 study. It is also intended to contribute to on-going OECD "horizontal" work on Sustainable Development – in particular, to the work examining the effects of subsidies and natural resource pricing policies on environmental sustainability.

The broad objective of this paper is therefore to summarise new developments and trends in water pricing practices which have occurred over the last ten years in OECD countries. In relation to the information contained in the 1987 report, this study seeks to provide more detailed information about:

- the water pricing *policies actually in place* in different OECD countries, including the characterisation of "groups" of countries or sectors of the economy where particular practices are most predominant;
- *trends in pricing practices* occurring in various economic sectors, especially the household, agriculture, and industry sectors; and
- *progress being achieved* toward the goal of more efficient, effective, and equitable water pricing practices in the OECD region.

The report is largely based on information presented in four recent background studies: an overview of water subsidies (OECD, 1997), and sectoral studies dealing with industry (OECD, 1999a), agriculture (OECD, 1999b), and households (OECD, 1999c).

13

The report is structured as follows. Chapter 3 provides an overview of the changing context of environmental pressures and conditions relating to water usage. It also discusses how water pricing can help fulfill some of the economic, social and environmental criteria necessary for sustainable development. Chapter 4 reviews the broad changes in institutional frameworks relating to water management in OECD countries, at both the national and international levels. Chapter 5 presents the existing water tariff structures and prices for domestic, industrial, and agricultural water consumption which are applied in the public (or quasi-public) water systems in OECD countries. Chapter 6 focuses on the charges levied on large water users for direct abstractions from watercourses. Chapter 7 then reviews water disposal charges, for both sewerage and sewage disposal to the public system, and for direct discharges into water systems. Chapter 8 examines the extent to which water supply and disposal systems in Member countries cover their operating and capital costs through these pricing structures – in effect, examining the prevalence of "subsidies" to water service users. Chapter 9 presents the available evidence about how water pricing structures and levels affect the demand for water services. Chapter 10 discusses issues of access to, and affordability of, public water supplies, and the social tariffs that can be used to address these problems. A few general conclusions are then presented in Chapter 11.

Chapter 3

Context

3.1. Demand for water

Abstractions of freshwater resources vary widely across OECD countries. Figure 1 illustrates the levels of annual *per capita* abstractions.[1] Unsurprisingly, apart from the US and *Canada*, both of which exhibit particularly large *per capita* abstraction rates, the highest abstractions are mainly found in countries with hotter climates (**Australia, Mexico,** and **Southern Europe**).

To some extent, the different abstraction rates also reflect the differing sectoral structures of OECD countries. These place very different demands on the water supply system. Figure 2 illustrates this variability. For example, the proportion of water abstracted for industrial uses varies from a maximum of 66 per cent in **Austria,** to a minimum of 3 per cent in **Mexico.** Similarly, the share of water used in agriculture varies from 77 per cent in **Turkey,** to 2 per cent in **Germany** and the **Czech Republic.**

On average (for the OECD countries in this sample with sufficient data), water used for industrial purposes (including power production) represents the largest share of water use (65 per cent, including 44 per cent for power and 21 per cent for industry), followed by agriculture (at 30 per cent). This situation is considerably different from world-wide statistics, which find the agricultural sector responsible for 69 per cent, and industry for 23 per cent, of total water withdrawals (UNIDO, 1996).

Different sectors also require different qualities of water with, for example, few industrial processes other than in the food and drinks industry requiring water of potable quality. While industrial water drawn from the public water supply (PWS) system is delivered through the same system as domestic water in most OECD countries (and is therefore of potable quality), irrigation water, as well as industrial water abstracted directly from the water course, generally are not.

The rest of this chapter examines in more detail the water demands of each of the household, agriculture and industry sectors individually.

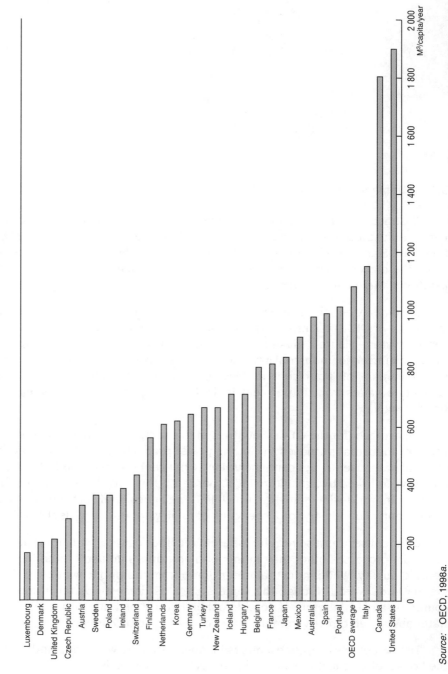

Figure 1. **Annual *per capita* Abstractions of Freshwater Resources in OECD Countries (Mid-1990s)**

Source: OECD, 1998a.

16

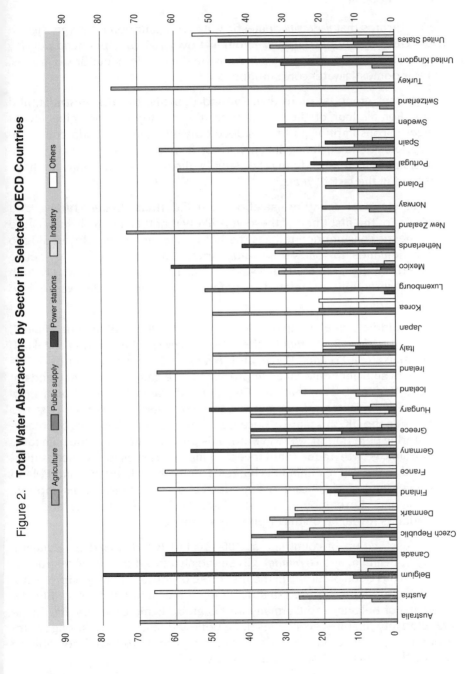

Figure 2. **Total Water Abstractions by Sector in Selected OECD Countries**

Source: OECD (1999a).

Household water demand

Table 1 indicates that *per capita* domestic water consumption rates vary significantly across OECD Member countries – from just over 100 litres per head per day (lhd), to more than 300. Countries can generally be divided into four broad groups, based on their domestic water consumption:

- A "high-use" group, at more than 250 lhd (**Canada**, the **US**, **Australia**, and **Japan**). For all four of these countries, the evidence concerning recent changes in consumption patterns is decidedly thin, but in Canada, consumption appears to be declining. In Japan, there is no evidence that average consumption has increased during the 1990s, while in Australia, it may not have increased in the last 20 years.

- A small group of countries, at about 200 lhd (**Italy**, **Spain**, **Turkey**, and **Sweden**). For the first three of these, it is likely that this relatively high figure for domestic consumption reflects the hot local climate (thereby leading to higher demands for showering and garden use). In Sweden, evidence collected for the 1987 study suggested that that country's relatively high water consumption was related to personal washing and dishwasher use (OECD, 1987*a*).

- A large "middle-range" group of countries, at 130-190 lhd (**Denmark**, **Finland**, **France**, **Austria**, **Switzerland**, the **UK**, **Norway**, **Luxembourg**, **Poland**, **Netherlands**, **New Zealand**, **Korea**, and **Ireland**). Of the nine countries in this group with sufficient data for an impression to be gained of recent trends, it is interesting to observe that only England and Wales (UK) and Korea show any underlying increase in domestic water consumption over the past two decades. In the UK, this may be because of the relatively low rates of domestic metering penetration, while in Korea it is probably linked to the high rates of economic growth, to the (until recently) high subsidies to water consumption, and to the use of minimum charges. Denmark, Switzerland, and Poland all show signs of significant recent decreases in *per capita* consumption. Finland and Luxembourg reveal slight reductions. France and the Netherlands reveal no distinct trends in recent years.

- A "low-use" group of countries, at 100-120 lhd (**Czech Republic**, **Hungary**, **Portugal**, **Belgium**, and **Germany**). Given the significant economic restructuring which has been occurring in the first three countries of this group, it is not surprising to find water use rates declining there during the 1990s. But the presence of Belgium and Germany in this group is more interesting. These are relatively "mature" economies, long believed to have had "strong" water economy policies for households, yet they still seem to have been able to reduce their consumption rates in recent years.

OECD 1999

Table 1. **Estimates of Per Capita Household Water Consumption**

Litres per *head* per day (lhd)

	1970	1975	1980	1985	1990	1991	1992	1993	1994	1995	1996	1997
Australia		256[1,2]	285[3,4]								268[5]	
Austria			155[6]							162[6]	133-5	
Belgium	72	93	103	108	116					120		122
Canada[7]		255[1]			350				350		326	
Czech Republic		138[1]	157[4]	165[8]			137			121		113
Denmark				175[8]	165	164	159	155	149	145	139	
Finland			148	155		150					145	
France (HH&SB)		106	109	141		161		157		156		
(HH only)												137
Germany[9]		133	141	145		144		136	132	132	128	129
(HH&SB)	118											
(HH only)	106	120	127	130		130		122	119	119	115	116
Greece[10]										140		200
Hungary	122	124	133	153	153	140	136	126	119	113	107	102
Ireland									142			
Italy			211					251		249		213
Japan	212	245	244	260	279	278	278	277	278	278		
Korea		62	69	103		160	164	169	181	175	181	183
Luxembourg			177	172	181					169		170
Netherlands				122	130	128	129	125	128	129	130	
New Zealand			170[7]	165[11]								
Norway			154	175								140
Poland			204	214	210					180	158	
Portugal									119			
Spain		145	157	158				210				
Sweden	229	207	196	195	197	195	201	203	199	191		
Switz. (HH&SB)	270	258	229	259		260				237		
(HH only)				180						158		
Turkey (PWS)[12]	105	113	136	159	182					195		
UK:												
– England and Wales												
(Unmetered)	106	114	122	129	136	137		142	147	154	149	153
(Metered)									131	134	132	141
– N. Ireland				136								
– Scotland			119[4]			148						
United States		295[1]	305									

Note: HH&SB = Households plus small businesses; HH only = Households only.
1. Estimate applies to 1997.
2. Estimate for Melbourne.
3. Estimate for Perth.
4. Estimate applies to 1982.
5. Urban domestic water use only.
6. HH and SB.
7. Source: OECD (1987b).
8. Estimate applies to 1987.
9. HH only estimate derived as 90% of HH and SB figure, following discussions with R. Stadfeld, BGW, Bonn. 1970-85 estimates: Old Länder. 1991-97 estimates: Old and New Länder combined.
10. Athens only.
11. Metered consumption only.
12. Per capita consumption of PWS including 68-70% household use, 23-27% public + commercial + offices, and 5-7% industrial.
Other sources used were IWSA (International Water Supply Association) statistics and numerous country submissions covering recent years.

OECD 1999

Industrial water demand

Industrial water use from the public water supply system has tended to decline in the majority of OECD countries over time. While the data gathered for this report does not show any significant trends across all OECD countries, some changes can be identified for individual countries. For example, a decreasing trend can be found in the former **West Germany,** where industrial abstractions through the public supply have fallen by one-third since the 1970s, as some industrial branches (such as chemicals, textiles, pulp and paper, and metallurgy industries) have made substantial efforts to reduce their water consumption. Other countries have shown a similar pattern of reduction in industrial water consumption, including:

– **Sweden,** where there was a sharp decrease in consumption from the PWS between the 1970s and 1980s, and a slow decrease from then on – with a 78 per cent decrease overall between the 1970s and 1990s.

– **Austria,** where industrial water use fell by 8 per cent between 1989 and 1991.

– The **Czech Republic,** where water use by industry declined by 40 per cent between 1985 and 1993, and water use by power stations went down by 20 per cent, while water use by the public supply system as a whole remained roughly the same.

– The **US,** where self-supplied water used by industry declined by 37 per cent between 1970 and 1990.

Box 1.   Defining Industrial Water Use

There are a number of difficulties involved in gathering data on the share of water used by industry, mainly due to difficulties in defining "industry". This term is not used in the same way in all OECD countries. For instance, commercial users (such as shops) may be included under "industry" in some countries, but not in others. More importantly, the category "industrial use" may include power production in some countries, but not in all. This is especially significant given that considerable volumes of water are *abstracted* for power production purposes, but there is a very low *consumption* rate for this use (because most of the water abstracted from the water course is then returned to it).[2] Similarly, some estimates of industrial use (and power production) include marine water use, while others do not. Moreover, defining the share of publicly-supplied water which goes to industrial users is often difficult, since the category "industrial use" usually refers to direct abstractions only. Therefore, it is likely that industrial consumption is under-estimated in some cases, because "public supply" usually includes supply to some industrial users as well.

In **Canada,** manufacturing water use increased between 1972 and 1981, but fell substantially from 1981 to 1991. In some countries, the recent reductions in *industrial* water use has sometimes been counter-balanced by increases in water abstractions for *power production.* In **France,** for instance, industrial water use declined from 16 per cent of total water use to 9.7 per cent over the last 15 years, but water use for power production increased from 25 per cent of total usage in 1981, to 63 per cent in 1994.

These decreases in industrial water consumption can be explained by several factors. First, industrial users appear to be more sensitive to price increases than domestic consumers (*i.e.* they have a higher elasticity of demand in response to price changes). Industrial users also have more options available for reducing consumption through the adoption of water saving technologies, in order to reduce costs. In some cases, they have been influenced by specific government programmes aimed at conserving water and/or reducing industrial pollution levels. This is the case in **Italy,** for example, where there has been a specific reduction in water demand by industry as a result of the adoption of water recycling and cleaner technologies, as influenced by the introduction of pollution control policies in 1976. Another interesting trend in this respect is the increase in water recycling by industrial users that has been taking place in various OECD countries, and can be observed in, for example, **Canada.**

On the other hand, industrial abstractions have also shown a clearly increasing trend in other countries or particular economic sectors. By 1994 in **Japan,** for example, the use of freshwater by the chemical industry had risen by 16 per cent relative to the 1980s, and by 3 per cent in the steel industry. In the **UK,** industrial use went up by 37 per cent between 1991 and 1995. In **Ireland,** industrial water use also increased during the 1980s, largely due to accelerated industrial development. Finally, in **Denmark,** industrial water use increased by 85 per cent between 1970 and 1988, although industry's share of total withdrawals remained roughly stable, at 28 per cent.

The importance of changes in industrial *structure* over time (*i.e.* from heavy industry to smaller and more technically-sophisticated industries) is more difficult to analyse. The de-industrialisation process in **Italy,** especially in the heavy industry sector, seems to have played some role in the reduction in industrial water demands there. In the **Netherlands,** the Association of Water Suppliers (VEWIN) forecasts that water use by large industrial users should decline up to the year 2000, but that consumption by the small business sector should increase.

Information on the major types of industrial water use was not available for all OECD countries. However, the industrial sectors with the largest water needs appear to be the chemical industry, the steel, iron and metallurgy industry, the pulp and paper industry, food and drinks, and oil and petroleum industries. Table 2 illustrates the relative share of each industrial sector within the manufacturing (or processing) sector, excluding power production.

Table 2. **Types of Industrial Water Use, Excluding Power Production**

As a Percentage of Total Industrial Water Use

	Chemical	Steel and iron	Pulp and paper	Food and drinks	Mining	Oil and petroleum	Textiles	Other
Austria	Together: 80			n.a.	n.a.	n.a.	n.a.	20
Belgium	18	43	15	4	14	n.a.	n.a.	6
Canada	21	22	38	8	1	6	1	3
Finland*	18	8	71	1	1	1	0	0
Germany	36	10	6	n.a.	26	n.a.	n.a.	n.a.
Hungary	18	27	n.a.	17	19	n.a.	n.a.	19
Italy	38	11	14	13	n.a.	2	7	15
Japan	32	25	10	n.a.	n.a.	n.a.	n.a.	33
Mexico^	17	5	5	46	0	12	1	14
Netherlands	59	9	2	7	0	21	0	2
Poland	28	13	8	9	11	3	3	25
Portugal	5	7	26	7	3	n.a.	45	7
Sweden	24	19	42	n.a.	n.a.	n.a.	n.a.	15
Turkey^^	7	10	14	28	8	4	17	12

n.a. Not available.

* Marine (brackish) waters excluded. For distribution of industrial water use including marine waters, see OECD (1999a).

^ Sugar production (37%) is included in Food and Drinks.

^^ Beet sugar is included in Food and Drinks; fertiliser industry is included in Chemicals. Data are approximate and based on 1997 industrial production.

Agricultural water demand

Both the proportion of arable land which is irrigated, and the per cent of total water consumption attributable to agricultural production, vary considerably across OECD countries (Table 3). This is mainly because of differences in the relative importance of the agricultural sector, as well as differences in the structure of agricultural production in the various countries. Even in areas where irrigation systems are common, agricultural water demand is quite heterogeneous. For one thing, various agro-climatic characteristics influence these demands. In arid climates, irrigation water cannot be substituted for, and is essential for growing crops. In wetter climates, irrigation water reduces the risk implied by unexpected climatic events, but crop production is still possible without irrigation.

Table 3 also illustrates recent increases in the amount of irrigated land in OECD countries. Most countries show significant growth over the last thirty years, with the aggregate increase for the sampled countries being 61 per cent. On the other hand, there has been some stabilisation in the acreages attributed to irrigated farming in most OECD countries over the past ten years, and a few (**Canada, Japan**, and the **UK**) have even experienced reductions.

Table 3. **Irrigation Areas and Agricultural Water Abstractions in Selected OECD Countries**

	Irrigation acreage (1 000 ha)			Arable area in use (1 000 ha) 1993	Irrigation acreage (%)	Total abstractions (million m³) 1995	Agricultural consumption (%) 1995
	1961	1985	1993				
Australia	1 001	1 700	2 107	48 900	4	15 055	–
Canada	350	748	710	41 400	2	43 900	–
Denmark	40	410	435	2 600	17	887	16
France	360	1 050	1 485	19 200	8	40 641	12
Germany	321	470	475	12 400	4	46 300	–
Greece*	522	1 099	1 330	3 900	34	7 030	81
Italy	2 400	2 424	2 710	12 000	30-35	20-25 000	50-60
Japan	2 940	2 952	2 782	4 600	60	90 497	64
Korea	1 150	1 325	1 335	–	–	23 700	63
Mexico	3 000	5 285	6 100	24 400	25	73 674	83
Netherlands*	290	530	560	1 952	29	1 128	13
New Zealand	77	256	285	13 600	2	2 000	55
Portugal	620	630	630	3 200	20	6 880	60
Spain	1 950	3 217	3 453	20 500	17	33 288	72
Sweden	20	99	115	2 800	4	2 725	4
Turkey	1 310	3 200	3 674	27 115	15	35 100	69
UK	108	152	108	6 700	2	11 752	1
US	14 000	19 831	20 700	189 900	11	470 000	64

* The statistics for the Netherlands and some for Greece refer to the area "sprinkled", rather than to the standard irrigated area.
Sources: Redaud (1997) and Raskin *et al.* (1997).

3.2. Environmental effects of water use

All OECD countries currently abstract less than 50 per cent of their annually available water resources (Figure 3).[3] Not surprisingly, countries with warmer climates, or those which are particularly dry, tend to abstract a larger percentage of their available resources. While this level of abstraction on its own is not especially worrying from an environmental perspective, the rate of increase in extraction rates does give cause for some concern in a few countries. **Turkey** and **Korea,** in particular, have increased their extractions of total available renewable supplies by over 5 percentage points since 1980. Conversely, some countries have been moving in the opposite direction, with the **Czech Republic, Denmark, Spain,** and the **UK** each having reduced their water abstraction rates by over 5 percentage points.

Such aggregate data, however, often mask important regional, local, or seasonal scarcities. For example, large urban areas and the existence of water-intensive industrial or agricultural centres can result in large local demands, with associated supply difficulties.

OECD 1999

Figure 3. **Freshwater Abstractions in Selected OECD Countries**

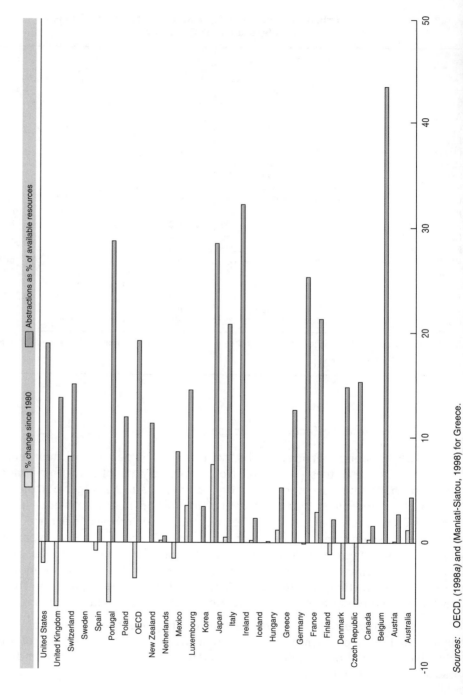

Sources: OECD, (1998a) and (Maniati-Siatou, 1998) for Greece.

Where farmland is maintained in areas where water is scarce, water problems resulting from irrigation may occur. Where irrigation involves pumping groundwater for local use, this can increase evapotraspiration of water, with a resulting net loss of water to the local or regional environment. As a consequence, water-based eco-systems, such as wetlands or forests, can suffer degradation. Thus, the draining and conversion of wetlands to other land uses (*e.g.* agricultural or urban development) can also result in significant environmental problems. This can lead to a loss of the wetland ecosystem, and to species loss. In addition, the reduced capacity for water storage will speed up water run-off and water through-put, which may, in turn, increase flood levels, and reduce the self-cleaning capacity of aquatic systems.

Irrigation water can also be transferred from one region to another. Environmental degradation associated with water withdrawal may then occur in one region, while other problems associated with irrigation itself may occur in the receiving region. The increasing intensification of farming practices in most OECD countries has generally contributed to the use of larger quantities of agricultural water in those countries.

Even where water shortages are not a serious problem, water quality (another type of shortage) often is. Water quality can be reduced both through direct pollution to water bodies and through an intensification of the mineral and salt content of water where excess abstraction occurs. For example, irrigation water usually contains some minerals in solution, which – depending on climatic conditions, soil types, crops, and irrigation patterns – can be deposited in the soil, reducing its reproductive capacity. Similarly, water percolating into the ground can be high in salt content, leading to a deterioration of local groundwater resources.

Intensive irrigated farming in semi-arid and arid areas can also lead to pollution of water bodies. Crops are often grown in areas (and in climates) to which they are not well-suited, and the use of agro-chemicals that are dangerous to the aquatic environment may be increased in order to regulate crop growth and protect against pests. These chemicals can run off into surface waters or percolate into the ground, causing significant damage to water quality. Intensive animal production may also lead to increased quantities of solid and liquid manure, whose disposal can negatively affect water quality.

Conversely, water-related agricultural activities can also have positive effects on the environment. For example, the cultivation of rice paddy fields in upland areas can reduce water runoff, prevent flooding in lowlands and limit soil erosion (Yoichi, 1992, as cited in Batie, 1997). Improvements in farm management techniques can also have a positive effect on both water quality and water demand, relative to more traditional practices. New techniques which employ less water, or allow more moderate use of pesticides and fertilisers, will reduce the runoff of

25

these chemicals into water bodies, while more efficient irrigation will lessen the pressure these activities have on the amount of water that is used. The maintenance of wetlands and improved soil management practices can also reduce erosion and enhance downstream ecological quality. Water pricing practices that encourage these conditions can therefore sometimes lead to environmental improvements.

In many countries, industry is the largest polluter of water resources, although its impact on the aquatic environment varies considerably, particularly with respect to the types and quantities of substances released. Because of their often large operational scales, industrial sites can be important point sources of pollution. Industry (e.g. thermal power generation) can also result in environmental degradation through thermal pollution. Heating aquatic ecosystems reduces dissolved oxygen while accelerating oxygen-demanding biochemical processes. In extreme cases, this combination can result in losses of fish life.

Available evidence for OECD countries (OECD, 1998d) suggests that there has been some progress in recent years in reducing discharges of "point source" industrial and urban pollutants into water courses; and in cleaning up the worst accumulations of water pollution that had previously been discharged. Conversely, there has not been enough progress in arresting "non-point" pollution (especially that from the agriculture sector, and especially pollution to groundwater reserves).

3.3. Links to sustainable development

Water pricing is an important element of water management, which in turn is an important element of environmental management. Water pricing is also a key component of the "water economy" in a given location, and can generate both problems and solutions for various social issues that may arise in the water management process (e.g. poverty). Because of its implications for the achievement of environmental, economic, and social goals, the implementation of appropriate pricing structures and levels for water services is an important element of the search for "sustainable development".

Where inappropriate water pricing systems are in place, therefore, it is not just the environment which suffers, but also the economy and society-at-large. Often, these effects will be inter-linked, and the effects of one will rebound on the others. For example, several OECD countries experience periodic water supply shortages, based on high levels of leakage in the water supply systems, or inefficient water usage encouraged by insufficient pricing policies. In addition to the environmental wastage of the water resources that leads to these shortages, the shortages themselves can ultimately affect both the health of local populations, and the profitability of industries which depend on water use.

Economic links

The scarcity of water resources leads to competing demands for its services, both among different sectors (and geographic areas) at a given time, and between different generations over time. Viewed from the perspective of economic efficiency, sustainable development implies that available water resources will be allocated to their highest-valued uses, particularly as supplies become constrained. Until recently, water providers relied largely on supply-management techniques to cope with increased water demands, either by expanding supplies, or by reducing inefficiencies in the supply of water services. The 1987 OECD study (OECD, 1987a) noted that pricing was increasingly being recognised as an important tool for influencing consumer demands as well. This emphasis on demand factors has several economic dimensions.

First, unless water prices reflect the long-run marginal costs of supply and distribution, water will tend to be overused by those economic sectors which add relatively less to economic output (or underused by those which add relatively more). This can lead to economic inefficiencies. Similarly, setting appropriate water prices will have a "dynamic efficiency" effect, in that the application of higher prices for water use will encourage the innovation and adoption of new water-saving technologies and processes.[4]

Appropriate pricing of water resources is also a key factor in maintaining the operational capacity of water supply/disposal infrastructure. Making water users pay for the costs they impose on public and private suppliers contributes to restraining demands – demands which would otherwise require costly new infrastructure investments.

In theory, a pricing system whose charges are equal to the marginal costs of providing the water services will allocate resources most efficiently. Such a system would ensure that the price charged for any particular water use reflected the incremental costs to the community of satisfying marginal demands. These incremental costs would include (both quantitative and qualitative) resource depletion/pollution costs, as well as the various capital and operating costs associated with infrastructure facilities.

In practice, deviations from the principle of marginal cost pricing are normal. These deviations are due to several factors. First, marginal cost pricing requires the measurement of actual water use by each customer, but individual water metering systems needed for this type of measurement are not always available. For example, domestic water meters – generally necessary for effective marginal cost pricing system – have not yet been installed in a number of areas, sometimes because of the initial investment costs involved, but also often because of the large on-going administrative expenses associated with reading these meters, and with making effective use of the data they generate.

27

Second, the implementation of proper marginal cost pricing may be so complex that the system is too difficult to administer, or incomprehensible to the consumer. Without customer understanding and acceptance of the system, it will inevitably be more expensive to implement, and (crucially) any demand-management incentives for water conservation could be misinterpreted. If consumers do not fully understand the system, they may either not respond rationally to the conservation signals that it contains, or they may react negatively to it. Third reliable and broadly-accepted monetary estimates of water pollution damages (or the opportunity costs of using water resources) do not exist. As such, setting prices to cover these costs, let alone applying them, cannot be done with a very high degree of accuracy.

Despite these limitations, a number of water pricing tariff structures are being developed in OECD countries which work towards the goal of marginal cost pricing, while still being cost-effective and simple enough to administer successfully. In addition to ensuring a tariff structure that is efficient, water utilities in most OECD countries are increasingly required to raise through water charges all of their ongoing operating costs, and to service some (or all) of the debt associated with their capital expenditures.[5] Where users do not pay the full costs of their use of water services, the public budget typically has to provide the difference. This is increasingly unacceptable in many OECD countries.

Social links

Adequate pricing implies that society as a whole will be able to capture any economic gains that may accrue from allocating the water, rather than allowing individual users to profit from their unique position in the water market. In effect, the rents from public resources should be captured by the public-at-large. Similarly, pricing is often used to contribute to social objectives related to poverty, inasmuch as minimum levels of water are often supplied to households, regardless of income levels, on the grounds that water is a basic necessity for life, and can therefore not be allocated solely on the basis of economic criteria.

Two notions of equity are important in the water pricing problem. First, there is the question of the general income distribution in the community – a matter for government policy as a whole. Second, there is the problem of how to construct an equitable system of charges with regard to the specific water services received by (or costs imposed on) consumers. The latter (more narrow) notion of equity raises important questions about cross-subsidisation from one group (or generation) of customers to another. The setting of rates, as well as the imposition of regulatory conditions on access to water services, can each result in discrimination in favour of (or against) certain water users or classes of users. Effectively, the result may be "cross-subsidies".

In addition to designing tariff structures which allow some cross-subsidies between different user groups, many OECD countries also rely on direct transfers (through non-full cost recovery) to water utilities, in order to ensure that customers receive reduced (affordable) prices for water services. It is increasingly recognised, however, that the general (and untargeted) under-pricing of water services is a fairly inefficient way of ensuring that low-income users have access to basic water services. Under-pricing also leads to over-consumption of the water resource, thereby threatening environmental objectives. As a result, most countries now offer special exemptions or discounts, that are targeted toward those consumers most in need of the price reductions.

In addition to targeting specific groups in society for price reductions, tariff structures can themselves often be designed to ensure that basic water services are affordable to all users. Increasing-block pricing is one way in which this goal can be achieved. This particular structure specifies that the costs per unit of water used increase the more water is used, thereby encouraging the conservation of water resources, as well as ensuring that low-income users pay less (on average) per unit of water than those (high-income users) which consume more.

Environment links

Although there are some specific situations where water usage is anticipated to result in *positive* environmental externalities (*e.g.* flood control and countryside management benefits), most of the anticipated externalities will be *negative*. These negative externalities will result from both the abstraction and supply of water and from the lack of adequate sewage treatment. They will thus involve both *quantity* effects (via the consumption of quantities of water resources in excess of natural replenishment rates – *i.e.* the unsustainable use of the renewable resource) and *quality* effects (via reductions in the quality of water bodies as a result of pollution). Environmental externalities associated with water supply occur, for instance, when the water table in a catchment area is lowered, affecting vegetation cover and surface water flows. Nutrient removal (phosphorus and nitrogen) must often be carried out to avoid eutrophication.

The negative externalities associated with insufficient access to waste treatment and public water supply are very important in terms of public health. For example, if sewage services are ineffective in removing human wastes from an urban area, the spread of communicable diseases may follow. Such diseases affect not only those without access to normal sanitation facilities themselves, but (because of their infectious nature) can go on to affect the larger community. The water supply system involves similar externalities, especially if local wells carry a risk of infection.

The public health criterion therefore requires that the whole population have safe and reliable access to an agreed minimum level and standard of water services. Where members of the population are unable to afford this service by themselves, government intervention may be required to ensure that appropriate health standards are established and maintained.

To some extent, environmental protection, economic development, and social policy objectives related to water use can be simultaneously achieved via the implementation of an "adequate" pricing system. The existence of externalities (*e.g.* environmental irreversabilities) means that pricing systems will never be sufficient on their own to fully achieve all of these objectives, but pricing can make an important contribution to the policy mix that is eventually adopted.

An "adequate" pricing system should optimally reflect all environmental scarcities and externalities. Setting unit volumetric prices for water use at sufficient levels to cover long-run marginal social costs can help to limit the demand for water services, thereby reducing wastage of a critical natural resource. For example, volumetric pricing (particularly increasing-block volumetric pricing) can have a positive effect on reducing demand for water services, while extra strength sewerage charges can encourage reductions in both quantitative pollution levels and pollution strength.

Where environmental scarcities and pollution externalities are not reflected in water pricing structures, the costs of depleting or polluting these resources will be borne by the community-at-large, rather than by those who created the problem in the first place. This also contravenes the Polluter Pays and User Pays Principles (insofar as these Principles are broadly defined to include polluters/users responsibility for the externalities/scarcities imposed on others).

Chapter 4

Recent Institutional Developments

The institutional setting in which water pricing policies are developed and applied is critical to the success of these policies in terms of achieving the policy objectives discussed in the previous chapter. This institutional setting includes the legal and regulatory frameworks in place, as well as the standards and "generally accepted principles" underlying these frameworks. For example, acceptance of the Polluter Pays Principle at the institutional level can facilitate (and may even be necessary for) the implementation of policies to internalise the environmental costs of water pollution. Thus, the institutional frameworks underlying water pricing policies in most countries need to be continuously strengthened and/or reformulated to better achieve these policy objectives.

Several OECD countries have experienced significant institutional shifts in the last decade which provide the groundwork for the introduction and application of more efficient water pricing to better reflect the marginal costs of providing the water services. Some of these shifts are discussed below.

4.1. Evolution at the international level

Over the last ten years, there has been considerable evolution in the way the international community views water pricing policies, and in the role of such policies in the distribution and sustainable management of water resources. To a large extent, this evolution has paralleled changes in the way countries interpret both the Polluter Pays Principle (PPP) and the (related) User Pays Principle (UPP).

The Polluter Pays Principle was first agreed by OECD countries in 1972 as a way of encouraging countries to not subsidise investments necessary for firms to comply with pollution control regulations (including water-based regulations). The past ten years have seen a continuation of the gradual transformation of this Principle into a (more) general concept – one which would require polluters to also bear the full costs of the environmental *damage* that they generate (OECD, 1996). For example, in a 1991 Recommendation on the Use of Economic Instruments in Environmental Policy, the OECD accepted for the first time the idea that not only pollution prevention and control costs should be borne by the polluter, but also pollution damage costs:

> ... Council recommends that member countries... work toward improving the allocation and efficient use of natural and environmental resources by means of economic instruments so as to better reflect the social costs of using these resources (OECD, 1991).

It can also be argued that the PPP has gradually become more deeply embedded in environmental law over this 10 year period, having moved from being a simple statement of principle, to being formally embedded in various legal instruments. For example, the 1992 Maastricht Treaty contains a specific reference to the PPP in its text.

The User Pays Principle has also become more widely (and more deeply) accepted during the past decade, and the water applications of this Principle have expanded considerably (see Smets, forthcoming 1999). For example, the OECD formally adopted the UPP in its 1989 Recommendation on Water Resource Management Policies, by stating that:

> ... resource pricing should at least cover the opportunity costs of these [water] services: the capital, operation, maintenance, and environmental costs (OECD, 1989).

In short, the scope of both the PPP and the UPP has grown in recent years, especially in the water management sector. This expansion has also been associated with related developments within the international community. One such development was the Dublin Statement on Water and Sustainable Development in January 1992. Although recognising that water is a foundation of life itself, and should therefore be provided at least in the minimum quantities necessary to meet basic requirements, this Statement also recognises that individual users should not have the right to limitless quantities of cheap water. There remains a need to allocate water resources efficiently, and to run water services cost-effectively, while still taking account of the "social good" character of water. More specifically, Principle 4 of the Dublin Statement asserted that:

> ... water has an economic value in all its competing uses and should be recognised as an economic good (http://www.gwp.sida.se/gwp/gwp/dublin1.html).

In June 1992, the Rio Declaration on Environment and Development (United Nations, 1992) further recommended that:

> National authorities should endeavour to promote the internalisation of environmental costs and the use of economic instruments, taking into account the approach that the polluter should, in principle, bear the cost of pollution, with due regard to the public interest and without distorting international trade and investment (Principle 16).

Five years later, the UN General Assembly adopted a resolution (United Nations, 1997a) at the Rio+5 summit which also recognised both the scarcity of water resources and the benefits of using pricing mechanisms to allocate these resources more efficiently across different consumer groups, and through time. Specifically, this resolution recommended that:

> *Consideration should be given to the gradual implementation of pricing policies that are geared towards cost recovery and the equitable and efficient allocation of water, including the promotion of water conservation* (Article 34.e).

To some extent, this Recommendation reflected a shift in the perception of the international community from one that considered water pricing primarily as a way to internalise the social costs of pollution, to one in which pricing is also seen as a tool for ensuring the most efficient use of scarce water resources, with special consideration for the social and environmental concerns of distributional equity and water conservation.

The economic value of water resources was also stressed at the Fifth Session of the UN Commission on Sustainable Development in April 1997, which concluded that:

> *... [i]t is essential that economic planning incorporate the idea of water as natural capital whose services can be depleted, as in using up groundwater or polluting water sources* (United Nations, 1997b, Section III.5).

These latter priorities were most recently echoed at an International Conference on Water and Sustainable Development, held in Paris on 19-21 March 1998. Ministers and Heads of Delegations present at this Conference committed themselves to implementing the following guidelines (where appropriate and in the framework of national and local strategies, and taking into account each country's specific circumstances):

– Mobilise adequate financial resources from public and private sectors and, as an important part of that task, enhance the effective use of available resources.

– To this end, provisions for progressive recovery of direct service costs and overheads, while safeguarding low income users, should be encouraged.

– Both the polluter pays principle should be promoted, and user-pays systems should be encouraged, at national and local levels.

Finally, the European Commission has recently launched a process leading toward the approval of a Framework Water Directive (COM(97)49), applicable to all **EU** Member States (Box 2). Although still under discussion, one of the major objectives of this Directive would be full cost recovery, applied to all water users. If eventually adopted, this Directive would also exert some external pressure on those governments reluctant to undertake pricing reforms on their own. In addition, the realisation of the implementation timetables set by the 1991 EC Urban Waste Water Treatment Directive 91/271/EEC will probably mean the addition of new wastewater charges to water bills between now and 2005.

33

Box 2. European Union Framework Water Directive

The EU Framework Water Directive (European Commission, COM(97)49, with revision COM(98)76), represents an ambitious plan by the European Union to integrate several disperse pieces of Community legislation with direct or indirect relationships to water issues, as well as adding a few new objectives which had been neglected in the past. Although still under discussion, this proposal has generated considerable debate in EU Member States, and some elements of this debate bear special mention here.

One of the most controversial components of the draft Directive is the role assigned to water prices for achieving conservation of adequate water supplies. Essentially, the Directive's underlying philosophy is that the failure to make water users responsible for the complete costs generated by their use is a source of water misallocation – one which seriously jeopardises future generations' access to water. It follows, then, that the implementation of full cost recovery prices to all water users – including capital costs, environmental damages costs and scarcity rent components – would represent a significant step towards a more sustainable exploitation of water resources.

Although the draft Directive clearly states that cross-subsidisation between sectors should be avoided, it would allow Member States to guarantee access to basic volumes of household water at "social" charge rates. Likewise, Member States would be permitted to grant exemptions based on programmes that encompass the subsidisation of capital costs for infrastructure projects with environmental objectives, as well as for projects developed in regions entitled to Structural Funds. On the other hand, the Directive also states that any deviations from full cost recovery pricing should be explicit and transparent.

4.2. Evolution at the national level

Role of government

The government role in water management has been shifting in many OECD countries, from that of being the primary provider of water services, to that of being the creator and regulator of an operating environment which allows communities, the private sector, and non-governmental organisations to become more active in providing water supply and sanitation services themselves.

In the agriculture sector, for example, some countries have been shifting irrigation facilities out of the public sector, and into the control of local users. This is the case in **Turkey**, where the government developers of irrigation infrastructure (DSI) have significantly accelerated the rate of transfer of this infrastructure to local users. Prior to 1993, about 2 000 ha per year was being transferred; in 1998 alone, 140 000 ha was transferred.

There is some tendency for OECD water supply systems to evolve toward the formation of groupings of municipalities, in order to organise supply at a larger scale. This reflects a recognition that the provision of water services can be inefficient when there are too many independent water providers involved in the process (for example, **Italy** has 13 500 water networks serving 6 600 municipalities nation-wide.) Thus, some consolidation has been occurring in several OECD countries. In the **Netherlands,** for example, the number of water boards has been reduced from 129 in 1990, to only 66 in 1997. **Finland** has seen 21 regional water supply and wastewater systems established since the late 1960s, although small municipal systems still predominate.

Simultaneously, the degree of autonomy enjoyed by local water service utilities has been increasing. In **New Zealand,** nearly all local authorities have established Local Authority Trading Enterprises (LATEs) to take over service provision, while in **Finland,** nearly half of all municipalities have established (or are planning to establish) local authority-owned water companies, similar to those which have long existed in **Germany.** They also exist in **France, Austria, Switzerland,** and **Northern** Italy (although in France, it is no longer permitted to establish municipal enterprises, so the number of these institutions cannot grow any larger). Similar restrictions are also in place in Quebec, **Canada**). In **Scotland,** three public water authorities were established in 1995 (with appointed members) to take over the water services supply roles of nine regional and three island councils (which had previously been managed by local authority representatives). These new Authorities are being encouraged to seek private financing for capital investments.

In some cases, water services are organised at the regional level, such as in **Australia, Canada, Ireland,** and the **UK.** This can facilitate the planning process, especially when the service providers' area of distribution corresponds to a river catchment area, such as the river basin (Box 3).

Box 3.   **River Basin Management Institutions**

The various states and provinces of **Germany** were among the first to develop river basin institutions, mainly to respond to specific water management needs in the shipping, irrigation, and flood control policy areas. The approaches applied in Germany were then used as models for other countries. For example, the structures developed in the Ruhr, Emscher, and Lippe Basins were adapted to **France** in the 1964 Water Law, which established the *Agences de Bassin* in that country. The *Agences de Bassin* remain key players in the management of French water resources today. Similar institutions already exist in **Spain, Australia,** and **Hungary,** and are in the process of being introduced in **Mexico.**

35

In a small, but increasing, number of countries, independent economic regulators have been set up to regulate water prices on an autonomous basis (Table 4). The economic regulator is usually in charge of setting prices, but may also have other responsibilities, such as establishing service performance standards. Water price regulation is generally exercised at the national level, or at the next level down in decentralised structures. In most cases, water is not treated differently from other consumer goods, and water price regulation is carried out by the Ministry of Finance, or the government body in charge of price regulation in general. The regulator's independence is typically seen as an important element in this process, in order to ensure that decisions are not influenced by short-term political considerations, and that they are as transparent as possible.

In the **US,** State Public Utility Commissions regulate all privately-owned utilities in a given state. This approach is also taken in the recently-privatised **UK** system. A similar "multi-utility-regulator" approach is taken in some **Australian** states (*e.g.* Victoria, with its Office of the Regulator General). Nevertheless, in most OECD countries, the government continues to fill the role of economic regulator.

Recent developments in OECD water laws and policies

A wide range of recent government Acts, Decrees, Orders and decisions in OECD countries are also changing the institutional context in which water pricing is being carried out. For example, much of the radical reforms currently being implemented in *Australia* have been driven by the 1994 Council of Australian Governments (COAG) agreement to implement a Strategic Water Reform Framework (Box 4).

In the **US,** the Safe Drinking Water Act (SDWA, including the 1996 Amendments) – the enforcement of which is largely delegated to individual States – is often cited as a force driving toward higher prices for water services. Other cost-increasing factors include: *i*) the need to replace an ageing infrastructure; *ii*) the costs of meeting increasing demands for water; and *iii*) the historic under-pricing of water services (use of average historic costs; failure to create adequate replacement funds; deferral of capital improvements; and subsidisation by various levels of government).

Tariff structures are also being directly affected by recent legislative decisions taken in several other OECD countries. In **France**, the January 1992 Water Law attempted, *inter alia*, to reduce water wastage, while promoting improved equity between users. With these objectives in mind, it prohibited the use of "flat fee" tariffs, thereby ruling out both entirely non-volumetric schemes (rare in France in any case) and tariffs combining a fixed charge (covering a given volume of household consumption per period) with volumetric charging (on the remainder). Departmental *préfets* now have the power to grant derogations on a case-by-case basis

Table 4. **Summary of Existing Institutional Arrangements in OECD Countries**

	Public Supply	Ownership*	Management*	Economic Regulator	Environmental Regulator
Australia	Regional	Both	Both	Regional/Independent	Independent
Austria	Municipal	Public	Public	Municipal	Central govt.
Belgium	Inter-municipal	Both	Both	Federal govt (prices)	Regional
Canada	Regional	Public	Public	Provincial govt	Provincial govt
Czech Republic	Municipal	Private	Both	Central govt	Central govt
Denmark	Municipal	Public	Public	Municipal	Central govt/municipalities
Finland	Municipal	Public	Public	Municipal	Central govt
France	Municipal	Public	Both	Municipal	Central govt
Germany	Inter-municipal/Municipal/Regional	Both	Both	Municipal/Regional	Regional
Greece	Municipal	Public	Public	Central govt	Central govt
Hungary	Municipal	Public	Both	Central govt	Central govt/Independent
Iceland	Municipal	n.a.	n.a.	n.a.	Central govt
Ireland	Regional	Public	Public	Regional	Central govt
Italy	Municipal	Public	Public**	Central and regional govts	Central and regional govts
Japan	Municipal	Public	Public**	Central govt	Central govt
Korea	National/Regional	Public	Public	Central govt/Regional	Central govt
Luxembourg	Municipal	Public	Public	Municipal	n.a.
Mexico	Municipal	Public	Both	Central govt	n.a.
Netherlands	Municipal	Public	Both	Central govt/Regional	Central govt/Regional
New Zealand	Municipal/Regional	Public	Both	Central govt	Central govt
Norway	Municipal	Both	Both	Central govt	n.a.
Poland	Municipal	Public	Public	Central govt	Central govt
Portugal	Municipal/Regional	Public	Both	Central govt	Central govt
Spain	Municipal	Public	Both	Central govt	Central govt/Independent
Sweden	Municipal	Public	Public	Municipal	Regional
Switzerland	Municipal	Public	Public	Central govt	n.a.
Turkey	Municipal	Public	Public	Central govt	Central govt/Regional
UK (England and Wales)	Regional	Private	Private	Independent	Independent
US	Municipal	Both	Both	Independent	Independent

n.a.   Not available.
*   "Both" means that public and private ownership structures co-exist.
**   Private management exists, but is marginal.

Box 4.   The Strategic Water Reform Framework in Australia

In order to promote more sustainable and efficient natural resource use in Australia, a number of deficiencies in the water industry had previously been identified. These included charging policies that had often resulted in commercial and industrial users of water services paying more than their fair share of the costs of service provision, of asset refurbishment in rural areas, of service delivery inefficiencies, and of impediments to water being transferred from lower- to higher-value uses.

To address these shortcomings, the Strategic Water Reform Framework of 1994 agreed on a number of reforms in relation to charging (Sydney Water, 1998):

- the restructuring of tariffs in line with the principles of "consumption-based" (*i.e.* volumetric) pricing and full cost recovery;

- the reduction or elimination of subsidies which are "inconsistent with efficient and effective service";

- increasing the transparency of all remaining subsidies and cross-subsidies; and

- where service deliverers are required to provide water services to customers or customer classes at less than full cost, the cost should be fully disclosed and (ideally) paid to the service deliverer as a Community Service Obligation (*e.g.* by the State government which imposes the requirement).

Appropriate economic and regulatory bodies have since been (or are being) established, and independent state regulators have begun to determine medium-term price paths, assessing (*inter alia*) tariff structures and levels.

(*e.g.* in very small rural systems where metering may not be cost-effective). The 1992 law also allows two other exceptions: where water is particularly abundant, and in zones where there is a strong seasonal fluctuation in the number of inhabitants. Despite these "let-out" clauses, the result has been a decisive move in France towards one- or two-part tariff systems, without minimum consumption charges.

In **Denmark,** a recent government Declaration (No. 525, of 14 June 1996) imposes an obligation on water utilities to ensure that (as of 1 January 1999) all properties connected to the public water supply have a water meter installed. Furthermore, payment for water deliveries must be made via a combination of a fixed charge and a volumetric charge (*i.e.* utilising at least a two-part tariff).

Korea issued the *Comprehensive Water Management Countermeasures* in August 1996 in order to: *i*) achieve full cost recovery for water services; *ii*) pursue demand management objectives; and *iii*) generate extra funds for investment purposes. These measures have already had two significant effects: the widespread abandonment by local authorities of the standard tariff's basic rate (which amounted to a minimum consumption charge), and a sizeable shift from "two-part" to "increasing-block" tariffs.

In **Portugal,** Decree-Laws 379/93 and 319/94 provide a new framework for private companies to be involved in the provision of water services, and prescribe that charges for privatised services must be fixed at "economic levels" (with prior approval from the Ministry of the Environment and Natural Resources necessary for EPAL).[6] EPAL has become the model for six new water companies which will provide services to more than half the population. Concessions to private companies will also be facilitated by the new legislation, with ten such concessions already in existence. Significant downward pressures on tariff levels are expected as a result of these changes.

In **Italy,** Law 36/1994 sets out a framework for the reorganisation of the entire Italian water industry. It provides for both vertical and (partially) horizontal integration of the water cycle (abstraction + public water supply + sewerage + treatment + discharge) within "optimal management areas" that the 20 Regions are expected to delineate themselves. Associations of local authorities must then take on responsibility for organising water services – previously held by 8 000 individual municipalities – on an integrated basis. Law 142/1990 further requires that various organisational forms can be used to discharge this responsibility, including private or public companies, or contracting out. Under this new system, prices will be set so as to cover full long-run costs (including a reasonable return on investment), with a single charging method for the entire vertically-integrated water cycle. However, the actual implementation of this law – particularly for sewerage services – has been slow so far.

Privatisation and commercialisation of public water services

The introduction of pricing systems can facilitate the private sector playing a more important role in the development and utilisation of water resources. For example, privatisation can encourage (or deepen) the development of markets for water services, which can in turn make it easier for marginal social costs to be incorporated into pricing structures.

However, most water services involve "natural monopolies" and as such, the *political* possibilities for introducing markets into their management are somewhat limited. There are also *technical* limitations to privatisation. For example, because the capital expenditures involved in water supply systems are typically large in comparison with the marginal cost of connecting an additional user, it is uneconomic to build separate water supply or sewerage systems for only a small number of users. It may therefore be uneconomic to privatise only a portion of the existing water supply infrastructure.

39

Some degree of government regulation will therefore continue to be required, in order to ensure that no abuse of monopoly powers occurs, and that the "public good" dimensions of water policy are realised.

These factors notwithstanding, substantial privatisation (asset ownership and management) of public water infrastructure has recently been taking place in some OECD countries (most notably in the **UK**, but also in some parts of the **US**), and is under active consideration in others (*e.g. Czech Republic*). The privatisation of the UK water industry took place in 1989, in order to tackle the need for additional sources of finance, and to improve the efficiency and quality of services (Box 5).

Box 5.   Water Privatisation in the UK

In 1989, **England and Wales** embarked on a programme of substantial privatisation (asset ownership and management) of the piped water systems provided by the ten Regional Water Authorities. A water regulator (Ofwat) was set up to protect customers against abuses of monopoly power, to promote economic efficiency, and to guarantee a stable environment for investment. The privatisation of these services is reported to have contributed to:
 – a much more "businesslike" approach to the provision of these services;
 – several mergers on the public water supply side (39 companies have now been reduced to 28, if account is taken of the previous smaller private water supply-only companies);
 – three large and three " water-only" companies have entered into extensive multi-utility arrangements; and
 – the first experience with public water supply competition – and lower prices – for large industrial water-users.

Source: OECD (1999a).

Even where the public water supply system remains publicly-owned, service management is increasingly being delegated to private operators. This approach seems particularly well-suited to decentralised systems, in which municipalities see delegation as a useful way of overcoming their own lack of technical expertise and/or financial resources. In **France,** and in a growing number of municipality-based systems, service providers are permitted to decide whether they want to manage the service themselves (direct management) or to delegate this management to a private operator. Currently, "concessions" (*i.e.* the delegation of authority to private concerns) in France involve 75 per cent of public water supplies, but only about one-third of waste-water services. A variety of such systems have also been adopted in the **Czech Republic,** they are increasing rapidly in **Spain** (40 per cent of the population are already served by concessions) and in **Portugal** (ten concessions have been granted), and they are under active consideration in **Hungary** and **Poland.**

More traditional forms of direct (municipal or supra-municipal) or delegated public management remain the norm in **Belgium, Canada, Denmark, Greece, Korea,** and **Sweden,** and in some areas in **Austria** and **Italy** (although changes may soon occur in the latter). In **Ireland, Luxembourg,** and **Turkey,** local authorities still appear to be responsible for most piped water services. In **Japan,** local authorities are responsible for almost all water supply, with the majority of the population (90 per cent) receiving piped water services from 1 949 local authority organisations and only 11 privately-owned water companies. In **Australia,** a commercial approach to the "business" of water has been adopted, but so far without private shareholders.

Chapter 5

Public Water Supply

5.1. Tariff structures

Introduction

A wide range of water services are supplied to commercial enterprises and households in OECD countries, including:

– the provision of potable piped water supplies;

– the provision of non-potable piped water supplies;

– direct abstractions/withdrawals of water;

– the disposal and any subsequent treatment of effluents through a sewerage system; and

– the direct discharge of effluents into receiving waters.

The first two and the fourth of these services are generally considered to fall under the heading of the "public water supply system". Non-potable water supplies are the minor component of such systems, and are not provided in many areas.

There are several ways in which these services can be grouped together for billing purposes. *Connection* costs will generally be recovered via a fixed charge; *water supply* will either be covered via volumetric rating systems (if metering is available), via fixed charges (if it is not), or via some combination of the two. For domestic customers, sewerage and sewage disposal charges are often presented together with the input water supply, as a combined tariff. This is possible because water intake has been found to be a satisfactory proxy for the volume of sewage generated in households. For *industrial* users of public sewers, however, the characteristics of water borne wastes differ enormously from one discharger to another. As such, a charging system reflecting differentiated charges for specialised treatment of different industrial waste characteristics may often be justified.

43

Basic tariff structures

A *tariff* system contains several elements which determine a customer's total water bill. These elements can consist of charges, measured in money/time units or money units alone. Unit prices are generally referred to as "rates", and are typically measured in either money or volume units. Most water tariffs are therefore a combination of some or all of the following elements:

– A *connection charge* is a "one-off" and (normally) "up-front" charge for connecting a customer to the public water supply and/or sewage system. Most OECD countries distinguish between connection charges (non-recurring) and fixed charges (recurring). The economic efficiency criterion suggests that this charge *not* be used to recover the general system development costs. To the extent that the latter are affected in the long-run by the scale of average or peak demands on the system, they are best recovered through a volumetric rate. Although it may be attractive for cash-strapped public (or profit-seeking private) utilities to secure capital contributions through connection charges, the result is likely to be the under-pricing of the final service. In the long-run, as domestic water use increasingly takes on (at least in part) the characteristics of a luxury service (power showers, swimming pools, garden use, etc.), under-pricing of the service will provide an environmentally-damaging and economically-misleading signal to consumers.

– A *fixed charge* (sometimes known as a *standing charge* or *flat fee*) is normally either equalised for each customer (*e.g.* within a given customer class or particular geographical location) or linked to some other customer characteristic (*e.g.* the size of supply pipe or meter flow capacity; property value; number of water-using appliances; lot size; etc.). In a metered environment, this charge should not recover more than " ongoing" customer costs which are not directly linked to the volumes of water used (*i.e.* those associated with a customer continuing to have access to the system, such as meter maintenance and reading, billing, and collection costs).

If a metering (measuring) system is in place, the following elements may also be found in the tariff system:

– A *volumetric rate*, which when multiplied by the volume(s) of water consumed in a charging period gives rise to the volumetric charge for that period. Economic and environmental efficiency both suggest that this element should recover all costs which vary with average or peak demands made on the system (in both the short- and long-run). There are several potentially complex issues here, having to do with the "fair" recovery of peak-related costs. However these issues may be resolved, the preference should be to seek recovery through volumetric charges, rather than via fixed ones. On the other hand, there are two possible reasons for recovering these costs through fixed charges instead. The first is to reduce the *financial risks* for the utility which might result from its exposure to the volatility of volumetric charges (however, a possible alternative is *minimum charges* – see below). The other arises if the costs of sophisticated meter technology and/or more frequent meter reading are perceived to be higher than the efficiency gains which derive from their use.[7]

– A *block charge*, defined by lower and (except for the highest block) upper volumes of consumption per charging period. Different volumetric rates are frequently attached to different blocks. If rates rise or fall consistently as more water is consumed, the schedules are referred to as *increasing-* or *decreasing-block* tariffs.

– A *minimum charge*, usually imposed to protect the utility's finances, which specifies that a certain minimum volume of the service will be paid for each period, whether or not that amount has, in fact, been consumed.

These are the key elements which constitute a tariff. Ideally, the tariff structure in any country will correspond to the principal(s) under which the pricing of water services is determined. Thus, if economic efficiency is one of the main priorities of the pricing system, volumetric rating of water consumption will often be utilised.

Theoretically, the individual water services provided should also be charged separately, rather than being "lumped" together. This allows consumers to be aware of the separate services involved, and to adjust their demands for each, according to the pricing signals being received. In practice, this is not always possible. For example, household *wastewater* services in most OECD countries are typically calculated on the basis of volumetric water *consumption*, and are therefore often included with the volumetric component of the water supply tariff.

Metering penetration

In order to apply marginal cost pricing, households and businesses need to be fitted with meters which can measure their individual water consumption. While almost all *industrial* enterprises are fitted with water meters in OECD countries, the same is not true for *household* users. The first column of Table 5 provides recent information on metering penetration in single-family houses in OECD countries. Twenty of the twenty-six countries mentioned in Table 5 meter all or nearly all (*i.e.* over 90 per cent) of single-family houses connected to the PWS. Some also have plans to extend their domestic metering systems in the near future. For example, the two largest remaining areas of unmetered charging in the *Netherlands* (Amsterdam and Rotterdam) are planning to complete their domestic metering activities soon.

On the other hand, there are no current plans to alter the unusual tariff policy in Antwerp, **Belgium** which obliges "high discretionary use" households to be metered, and gives all others a choice (a total of about 30 per cent were being

Table 5. **Metering Penetration in Single-family Houses and Apartments Connected to the PWS**

Per cent

		Metering penetration in:		
		Single-family houses	Individual apartments[1]	All individual households
Australia	1998	95-100	"insignificant"[2]	n.a.
Austria	1998	100	"very few"[3]	n.a.
Belgium	1997	90	"many cases"	n.a.
Canada	1998	55	"few"	n.a.
Czech Republic	1998	100	n.a.	n.a.
Denmark	1996	64	"1 in Copenhagen"	n.a.
Finland	1998	100	"very low"	n.a.
France	1995	100	> 50	88
Germany	1997	100	10-20	55-60
Greece[4]	1998	100	100	100
Hungary	1998	100	n.a.	n.a.
Iceland	1997	0	0	0
Ireland	1998	0	0	0
Italy	1998	90-100	"many examples"	< 30
Japan	1997	100	94	100
Korea	1998	100	100	n.a.
Netherlands	1997	93	n.a.	n.a.
New Zealand	1997	25	n.a.	n.a.
Norway	1998	"low"	0 or "very low"	10-15
Poland	1998	100	0	"about 10"
Portugal	1998	100	n.a.	n.a.
Spain[5]	1998	"nearly 100"	"nearly 100"	95
Sweden	1998	100	0	"about half"
Switzerland	1998	100	0	n.a.
Turkey[6]	1998	"nearly 100"	"nearly 100"	> 95
United Kingdom:				
Eng. and Wales	1998	12+	"a few"	11
N. Ireland	1997	0	0	0
Scotland	1997	"near 0"	"near 0"	0.002
United States	1997	90+	n.a.	n.a.

n.a. Not available.
1. This applies to cold water metering; hot water provided in apartments under district heating schemes is normally metered but even here, the practice varies widely.
2. "Insignificant" in Sydney only; the situation elsewhere is unknown.
3. It is estimated that "perhaps about 20" apartment buildings in Vienna have individual meters.
4. Athens only.
5. Barcelona only.
6. Ankara only.

charged by meter in early 1998). Indeed, in many countries, domestic metering is not a high priority issue. In **Ireland**, domestic metering has been considered, but has so far been judged uneconomic. In **Iceland**, there appears to be no serious consideration underway of the domestic metering option, and metering also seems to be spreading very slowly in **Norway**.

OECD 1999

In **New Zealand** and **England and Wales,** metering is a very controversial policy issue, largely because of its possible implications for low-income households (Box 6). Thus, two water companies in England (Anglian and Yorkshire) have had to withdraw compulsory metering programmes in the last few years, in the face of determined public opposition. OFWAT, the economic regulator of the privatised water companies in England and Wales, is formally opposed to universal domestic metering (on cost-benefit grounds), but supports compulsory selective metering: where new resources are scarce (and hence expensive); where households are con-suming significant amounts of "discretionary" water (e.g. for luxury use, especially garden watering); and for new homes where the initial installation costs are rela-tively low. All water companies also offer – with the regulator's approval – a meter-ing option, so that those households which use little water have the opportunity of paying a bill that reflects their (small) level of consumption.

Following the severe drought in 1995, many water companies in southern and eastern **England** now have expansionary domestic metering programmes underway. Anglian Water, one of the strongest advocates of metering, expects to have over 38 per cent of households metered by March 1999 and 60 per cent early in the next decade. This represents a significant increase on the 2.7 per cent that were metered in 1992. Cambridge Water, a smaller water-supply-only company within the Anglian area, plans to meter all of the 25 000+ hose-pipe users by the end of 1999, and expects to reach a 50 per cent metering penetration of its 100 000 households a few years later (Kay, 1998).

Unlike metering penetration for single-family houses, the situation in apart-ment blocks – where most of the population live in a significant number of OECD countries – is much more varied. A limited amount of information is provided in Table 5 concerning domestic metering in individual apartments. While the water being supplied to apartment buildings is metered in nearly all OECD countries, it is only in a few countries that separate metering is available for individual apart-ments. In most cases, the owner, manager, or some other responsible person receives a volumetrically-based water bill. Generally, these charges – together with those applying to wastewater services – are then recovered from residents by some criterion (such as m^2 of floor space, number of rooms, number of residents, appli-ance ownership, etc.).

There are essentially two reasons why pressures may exist for the metering of individual apartments: equity and efficiency. Equity concerns arise because, as the real cost of water to households increases, non-volumetric charging systems pro-mote more cross-subsidisation of the profligate/high water users by the economic/ low users. In other words, real income transfers that may already be perceived to be unfair become even larger. Requests typically follow (from the economic/ low-income subsidisers) for the installation of meters. But as long as the water

Box 6. Domestic Metering in Christchurch, New Zealand

Christchurch City was formed in 1989 from five separate local authorities. The pre-1989 Christchurch City Council area was fully metered, and had a system of consumption-based charging. This system used capital value ratings of houses to establish an initial allocation of water, and then charged by volume for usage above that allocation. Approximately 20 per cent of customers received bills for entering the tranche where volumetric charging occurred. The four other authorities in the new agglomeration had used metering only on their commercial and industrial properties. Residential services were unmetered and payment was made via either a property capital value charge or a uniform charge. Upon amalgamation, the new Council decided to return to capital-value-based rating for all domestic consumption, retaining a volumetric system for the other consumer groups.

Christchurch relies largely on groundwater abstractions from local artesian aquifers. Reports in the 1980s had already drawn attention to the possibility (and undesirable effects) of over-abstraction from these aquifers. In 1991, the new Council therefore resolved to complete the metering of the whole city. It was also decided at that time to delay finalising a decision on the particular tariff system that would be adopted until the installation programme was nearing completion. The metering programme was duly completed in 1996, with NZ$ 7 million having been spent on the project. Discussion began in 1995 concerning the details of the preferred charging system to be used.

In September 1996, the City Council resolved that volume-based charging should be recognised as one of the effective means of managing demands, but decided not to proceed as planned in the introduction of a volumetric charging system for all consumers. Instead, the Council decided to continue to implement a variety of other (non-volumetric charging based) water-saving strategies. In part, this may have been due to the already successful reported *per capita* demand reduction in Christchurch of 13 per cent between 1991 and 1996. This decline was estimated to be due to:

- reductions in commercial use due to the new tariff structures (2 per cent);

- the pricing system giving industry an incentive to switch from the public water supply to direct abstractions from the aquifer (not necessarily a positive effect from a water conservation perspective) (2 per cent);

- more leakage being discovered with the aid of domestic meters which, *although not being used for charging purposes*, continue to be read (4 per cent);

- new urban development, implying a larger built-up area and therefore less water being required for irrigation (3 per cent); and

- changes in public attitudes caused in part by the installation programme itself and by advising residents – especially large users – of the actual amount of their consumption (2 per cent).

utility recovers its aggregate charges, it can be argued that this equity issue is not its concern, but rather a problem to be addressed by the apartment block's owner him/herself.[8]

Second, there are *efficiency* reasons. Imagine a situation where water demands are increasing within some of the apartments (perhaps because of rising incomes), and where there are also significant local or regional resource constraint problems on the available water supplies. In this case, the presence of a single "master-meter" may have no effect on total demand (the owner allocates the increase in the aggregate bill between all the apartments, and each resident decides that the increase is not his/her fault, but pays the bill anyway). However, the objectives of economic efficiency and environmental sustainability both require a demand-side response in this situation. In order to generate such a response, appropriate pricing or other signals must be sent to those apartments responsible for the increased consumption.

For both of these reasons, some OECD countries have begun metering water use in individual apartments. In **Germany,** Kraemer and Nowell-Smith (1997) report significant moves since the 1980s to promote the metering of individual apartments, especially in Hamburg, Berlin, and Frankfurt. Two types of initiative are being observed. First, the local authority may be the prime mover. For example, the City of Hamburg began a programme to install individual meters in all flats in 1985, and (from 1987 onwards) all new and renovated apartment buildings in the city have had to have individual meters. By 2004, all households will have their own meters. Second, on a wider scale, the building codes of the Länder have begun to be amended to provide for the compulsory metering of individual flats in new buildings, as well as (sometimes) the incorporation of individual meters when old apartment blocks are being renovated. In Hesse, water abstraction taxes are being used to give financial support for retrofitting meters in these situations.

This policy change is less marked in most other European countries. Thus, in **Belgium,** owners or managers of apartment buildings have "in many cases" installed private meters in individual flats, and there is also a (slow) movement toward individual metering by the water companies.

In **France,** individual metering has always been relatively common. Already by the early 1970s, 50 per cent of apartments were being metered for cold water [OECD (1987*a*), Table 14]. Since 1974, all new housing units have had to be equipped with a meter for each flat. Barraqué and Cambon (1997) explain that this policy originated in the need to measure centrally-generated hot water, with this approach later being extended to include cold water, and eventually being generalised "at the request of managers of large condominiums, following increasing disputes between tenants" (*ibid.*). However, it should not be assumed that water utilities always read these meters, since they are often beyond legal access. The

49

number of meters in apartments appears to have grown significantly in France in recent years, with a 1995 survey finding that 88 per cent of households are now being metered individually.

In **Switzerland**, the allocation of water costs within an apartment building is seen as the responsibility of the owner, and there are no plans to take a more pro-active stance. As the price of water has become the subject of increased public debate in **Italy**, the collective metering of consumption has also given rise to more complaints about cross-subsidisation. Apartment residents normally have the right to ask for their own meter, but they must pay for its installation. The expansion of individual apartment metering is therefore occurring quite slowly.

Sydney Water (**Australia**) reports that it encourages the implementation of individual metering in apartment blocks, but is content to leave the decision to those responsible for managing the building, since it is usually more cost-effective – presumably viewed from the water utility's perspective – to charge for the building as a whole.

The situation in **Denmark** highlights the efficiency issue mentioned earlier. Recent Danish legislation requires that (as of 1 January 1999) all properties connected to the public water supply must be metered. The duty to commence installation rests with the water utility, although the cost must be met by the individual owner. The metering penetration of single-family houses is therefore expected to increase rapidly. In addition, provision must now be made for the "later" installation of individual meters in newly constructed apartment blocks, with a maximum of two feeder-pipes for each apartment (one for cold water, one for hot) (Box 7). What is meant by "later" has yet to be determined. There are no proposals to insist on retrofitting meters in old apartments, but planned legislation will permit water supply utilities to charge residents of apartments which have individual meters installed directly. However, this approach may lead to relatively complicated billing systems, and may prove difficult to administer as a result.

While water metering is increasingly common in the *domestic* sector of most OECD countries, and is almost universal for *industrial* users, it is still an exceptional procedure in most *agricultural* districts. The **UK** is an exception, with interest in *agricultural* water metering having increased significantly there, following the recent large-scale privatisation of water services (even though metering is still far from being a universal practice). In general, the metering of water use in agriculture is costly, and therefore sometimes inefficient. For example, Tsur and Dinar (1997) have estimated that, under quite generic conditions, if the cost of applying volumetric pricing techniques exceeds 10 per cent of the revenues collected through these charges, then simple area-pricing would usually be more efficient.

The fact that water is often rationed among users without metering should not, however, be interpreted as a situation in which property rights are poorly defined. Likewise, the fact that water is metered does not mean that it is either expensive

---

Box 7.   Metering of Apartments in Copenhagen

The situation in Copenhagen brings together a number of the issues raised above. Copenhagen has a serious groundwater pollution problem. In addition, Copenhagen's abstractions are threatening to mine the groundwater resources, with a consequent adverse effect on wetlands. Of the 288 000 households served by the public system, only 5 per cent live in single-family houses (all of which are metered). The other 95 per cent live either in apartments or in terraced houses. Of the 95 per cent of non-single-family-houses, only about 3 100 households (about 1 per cent) have individual meters, and all of these have been fitted as a result of individual choice. The Copenhagen utility therefore faces the problem of "forcing" the scarcity signal through to the 94 per cent of their households who at present do not receive this signal via a price on their water bills.

As a result, the utility has sought to expand the individual metering option, despite legal restrictions on this option. It is currently investigating the effects of introducing meters at the individual apartment level, with a view to reducing water consumption. The utility is also stressing the financial advantages which may accrue from individual meter installation, but, as yet, without offering the option to its clients of having a free meter installation.

---

or scarce. There are many examples illustrating that achieving water distribution and/or management goals need not involve metering approaches. In fact, appropriate signals about water scarcities can even be provided to users without water pricing at all (*e.g.* in *Japan* – see Box 10, discussed later). Admittedly, these cases stand out as exceptions, and they cannot be easily achieved unless the accompanying institutional arrangements are well-rooted and accepted by all participants.

Temporal tariff variations

Water demands, particularly for households and agricultural users, are unevenly spread over time, with demands generally being highest in hot and dry conditions. Other non-climatic factors and consumer habits also drive peaks over shorter time periods: both within-the-day and, to a limited degree, within-the-week. For example, households generally have diurnal water demands, with peaks occurring in the early mornings and late evenings. Engineers, economists, and environmentalists all have reason to be interested in such temporal variations, since large costs will be faced by water utilities if supply systems need to be constructed, maintained, and operated at a scale which can satisfy whatever peak flows may ultimately be demanded.

51

If charging systems can be designed and operated so as to even out demand patterns (perhaps by simply pricing some of the more luxurious peak demands out of existence), suppliers can reduce the capacity of their systems, thereby saving resources, lowering customer bills, and reducing the demands being made upon the environment. Pricing analysis to date has mainly concentrated on peak-hour, peak-day, peak-week, and peak-month demands, as well as on average demands in especially hot and dry years, and over longer dry periods. Over all these time periods, pricing may "compete" with storage as a way of reconciling supplies and demands. Least-cost planning then provides an appropriate intellectual framework in which to establish the most economically and environmentally efficient solutions (more storage, more demand management through extra tariff sophistication, or some combination of these approaches). Alongside these factors, the criteria of equity, technical feasibility, consumer understanding and acceptability, and risk all need to be considered before a final decision on tariff structures is made.

In practice, it has been found that tariff policies have the most to offer policy-makers in the temporal dimension in "time-of-day" and "seasonal" pricing. Other peak demands – for example, peak-day and peak-week – tend to be best handled within general volumetric charging or seasonal tariffs, rather than being granted their own extension to the temporal tarification system.

Household tariff structures

Recent information about the tariff structures for domestic water consumption currently in place in OECD countries is presented in Tables 6 and 7. Most of the data for Table 6 is expressed in terms of the distribution of populations (often according to number of households), sometimes in terms of the distribution of util-ities, and sometimes both. The Table 7 data on fixed charges in the public water supply is much "softer", largely because of the sheer complexity of those particular charging arrangements. Unfortunately, no survey data is available concerning the charging systems in place in individual apartments, because so few are metered.

As can be seen from these Tables, tariff structures for domestic water consump-tion vary significantly among OECD countries. While some countries rely entirely on flat fees (*e.g.* **Iceland, Northern Ireland,** and **Scotland**), others rely entirely on variable charges (*e.g.* the **Czech Republic** and **Hungary**). The majority of countries, however, use a combination of the two. Where flat fees or fixed elements are used in the tariffs, these may be charged at the same level for all households, or varied (depending on the lot, household, or garden size; the pipe or meter size; the num-ber of taps; or the number of rooms).

Although it is clear that considerable variation exists in OECD household tariff structures, there are some indications of a general shift towards more econom-ically efficient charging systems, better targeted social variations, and the

Table 6. Public Water Supply: Household Tariff Structures

% of Utilities (U) or Population (P) with a Given Structure

	Year	Number of utilities in sample	Unit	Flat fee	Constant volumetric rate			Increasing-block schedule			Decreasing-block schedule			Usual number of blocks
					No fixed charge	Plus fixed charge	Plus fixed +min	No fixed charge	Plus fixed charge	Plus fixed +min	No fixed charge	Plus fixed charge	Plus fixed +min	
Australia	1997	15	P(U)	–	1(1)	68(8)	–	–	27(5)	–	–	4(1)	–	2
Austria	1993		U	–	–	80	–	–	20	–	–	–	–	–
Belgium:														
Flanders	1997		U,P	–	–	← 24 →	–	–	100	–	–	–	–	2
Wallonia	1997		U,P	–	–	–	–	–	76	–	–	–	–	2
Brussels	1997		U,P	–	–	100	–	–	–	–	–	–	–	–
Canada	1996	1 452	U	56	–	← 27 →	–	–	← 4 →	–	–	← 13 →	–	2
Czech Republic	1998		U,P	–	100	–	–	–	–	–	–	–	–	–
Denmark	1998		U,P	Rural	–	Most	–	–	–	–	–	–	–	–
Finland	1998		U,P	–	–	100	–	–	–	–	–	–	–	–
France	1990	500	U	2	5	46	47	–	–	–	–	–	–	–
Germany	1998		U,P	–	–	100	–	–	–	–	–	–	–	–
Greece	1998		U	–	–	–	–	5	–	100	–	–	–	5
Hungary	1997	268	U	–	95	–	–	–	–	–	–	–	–	2
Iceland	1997	1	U	100	–	–	–	–	–	–	–	–	–	–
Ireland	1998			All domestic water charges have been consolidated into general taxation since 1 January 1997.										
Italy	1998		P	Yes	–	–	–	–	100	–	–	–	–	2-7
Japan	1998	1 900	U	–	–	–	42	–	–	57	–	–	1	6-10
Korea	1998		P,U	–	–	–	–	–	100	–	–	–	–	2-3
Luxembourg	1997		U	–	–	Yes	–	–	Yes	–	–	Yes	–	–
Mexico	1996		U	–	–	–	–	–	← 74 →	–	–	← 26 →	–	–
N. Zealand	1998		P	75	–	25	–	–	–	–	–	–	–	–
Netherlands	1996	28	P(U)	7(1)	–	90(25)	–	–	3(2)	–	–	–	–	2
Norway	1998		P	87	–	13	–	–	–	–	–	–	–	–
Poland	1998			–	–	Most	–	–	Most	–	–	–	–	–
Portugal	1996			–	–	–	–	–	← 90(321) →	–	–	← 0.2(3) →	–	2-5
Spain	1994	389	P(U)	–	–	← 10(65) →	–	–	–	–	–	–	–	3
Sweden	1998	288	U	–	–	100	–	–	–	–	–	–	–	–
Switzerland	1998		P(U)	–	–	95 (235)	–	–	5(1)	–	–	–	–	2
Turkey	1998		P(U)	–	–	–	–	–	← 100 →	–	–	–	–	3
UK:														
Eng and Wales	1998		P	90	–	10	–	–	–	–	–	–	–	–
N. Ireland	1998		P	89	–	11	–	–	–	–	–	–	–	–
Scotland	1998		P	100	–	0.002	–	–	–	–	–	–	–	–
US	1997	151	U	2	1	← 32 →	–	1	← 30 →	–	–	← 34 →	–	3

Table 6. **Public Water Supply: Household Tariff Structures** *(cont.)*

% of Utilities (U) or Population (P) with a Given Structure

Notes:

Belgium: Antwerp meters high water-users in the residential sector, and offers a choice to other households. In Flanders, following a regional decree which came into force on 1 January 1997, all utilities introduced a free allowance of 15 cubic metres per person per year (about 41 lhd). That is the reason all Flanders utilities are recorded as having an increasing block system. Without the free allowance, only two utilities would be recorded as having an increasing-block system: all the rest would in that case be classified as "constant volumetric rate plus fixed charge".

France: Old survey data. Water Law of 1992 ruled out (with some exceptions) a flat fee and constant volume rate + fixed + minimum charge. These categories are now in decline.

Germany: Some water suppliers apply a linear tariff with no fixed element for household consumption.

Greece: Athens only.

Iceland: Reykjavik only.

Italy: A very small fixed charge (meter rent) is applied, and (often) a free minimum allowance as well.

Japan: While Japanese utilities do levy a minimum charge (applicable for the first 10 m³, they do not levy a fixed charge.

Netherlands: Amsterdam is unmetered. Rotterdam and a few smaller water boards are partly unmetered. Most of these plan to meter all households soon. Two smaller water supply utilities offer metered households a free allowance (30 m³/year and 25 m³/year) before a single volumetric rate begins to operate.

Turkey: Information applies only to urban areas and metropolitan cities (covering 65 per cent of Turkey's population).

England and Wales, Scotland: A choice is offered to all households, except those living in new houses (which are generally metered when they are built) and i) users of garden sprinklers and swimming pools and ii) under some water companies, certain other selected groups of high-use houses or households are also compulsorily metered.

Apartments: There is no necessary consistency in the data concerning how individual apartments and apartment buildings are treated in different countries; the best presumption is probably that the percentage figures refer to single-family houses and apartment buildings. However, see Table 14 on metering penetration (below).

Table 7.   **Fixed Elements of PWS Tariff Structures for Households**

	Determination of Flat Fee (Ff) and/or Fixed Element (Fe) of PWS Tariff
Australia	Fe: equal, PV: meter size
Austria	Basic rate = metering charge, varying by pipe size
Belgium	Fe: Equal for each house, fixed by utility
Canada	Ff: equal, PV; property front, lot size
Denmark	Ff: PV, no. of taps, estimated volume; Fe: meter size.
Finland	Fe: equal (fixed by utility); Fe: meter size
Germany	Fe: equal (fixed by utility)
Greece	Fe: equal for all households (Athens)
Iceland	Ff: fixed charge + rated per m^2 of house (Reykjavik)
Ireland	Domestic charges consolidated into general taxation
Italy	Fe: "insignificant"
Japan	Basic Rate"= Minimum charge, varying by pipe size (45.3% of utilities) and/or user group equal for all households (for 41.4% of all utilities)
Korea	Fe: pipe diameter
Netherlands	Ff: by m^2 of house or by number of rooms or garden size; Fe: equal (fixed by utility)
New Zealand	Ff: based on PV, metered; Fe: equal
Norway	Area of house
Portugal	Fe: pipe diameter
Spain	Fe: size of meter
Sweden	Fe: size of meter
Switzerland	Fe: size of meter
Turkey	Fe: equal for all households, fixed by municipality
UK:	
Eng and Wales	Unmetered Ff: PV; Metered Fe: equal
N. Ireland	Ff: PV
Scotland	Ff: PV
US	Equal for each household, fixed by utility

Notes: PV = property value, rateable value of property, or some variant.
      Fixed elements for PWS and wastewatwer tariffs in some countries include annualised contributions to initial property connection charges.
Sources: Ecotec (1996); Ecologic (1996-98); Ecologic (1997-98) and numerous publications or other documents supplied by and/or relating to individual countries, and assembled for this project.

implementation of incentives for water conservation. Thus, there has been a general move away from fixed-price and decreasing-block tariff structures, and towards volumetric charging and increasing-block structures.

However, traditions in the water industry generally die hard, both in terms of the charging arrangements themselves, and in terms of the water industry's intellectual approach to solving its problems. In the **US** and *Canada,* for example, where thousands of municipalities have organised their own water affairs for many years, it is unsurprising that a wide range of different structures has evolved. In addition, water is perceived to be (and frequently is) very cheap in those countries, with past subsidies, historic cost accounting, and a failure to deal with the effects of externalities having accentuated the policy effects of large natural endowments of water. As a result, tariff structures in those countries have been slow to respond to the withdrawal of government funding in recent years, or to recognise emerging environmental problems.

A 1997 sample of 151 utilities in the **US** found the majority operating volumetric tariffs (34 per cent with decreasing-block tariffs, 33 per cent with uniform volumetric charges, and 31 per cent with increasing-block) while only 2 per cent applied flat fees (Raftelis Environmental Consulting Group, 1998). When compared with a 1982 survey (Lippiatt and Weber, 1982), this reflects a general reorientation of tariff structures over the last 15 years, with about 25 per cent of utilities appearing to have switched out of decreasing-block schedules, and into increasing-block ones (which offer stronger incentives to conserve water). However, change is slow – indeed, between late 1995 and late 1997, the recorded proportion of increasing-block schedules actually *fell* by 1 per cent.

Evidence from **Canada** (Table 8) is at first sight more puzzling, since the flat fee proportion of the total water bill appears to have increased over 1986-1996, whereas in other countries the flat fee has generally been decreasing. In part, this is caused by the large number of smaller utilities that have recently joined the sample (by responding to Environment Canada's occasional surveys). But even without these additions – which have a higher propensity to not engage in domestic metering – the tendency up until 1991 was for more flat fee charging, at the expense of the decreasing-block rate. Over 1991-1994, however, the position was reversed; indeed, analysis of municipalities with a population of over 10 000 (responsible for over 85 per cent of Canada's population) shows 52 per cent now charge their residential customers by some sort of volumetric system, up 4 per cent since 1991.

In both the **UK** and **New Zealand,** progress towards more "rational" pricing structures has also been held back by tradition, as well as by a genuine concern that any rapid shift to domestic metering (*e.g.* in the much drier south and east of

Table 8. **Piped Water Services: Domestic Tariff Structures in Canada (1986-96)**

Per cent

	1986	1989	1991	1994	1996
Flat fee	47	53	61	58	56
Uniform volume charge	23	22	22	24	27
Increasing-block	2	2	3	4	4
Decreasing-block	28	23	14	14	13
Total	100	100	100	100	100
Number of utilities in sample:	(591)	(732)	(1 416)	(1 508)	(1 452)

Source: Environment Canada, various publications.

England) would cause undue financial hardship on low-income households with children. As noted earlier, two large water companies in England – Yorkshire Water and Anglian Water – have recently withdrawn or modified household metering expansion programmes for exactly that reason. However, about 3 per cent of households are switching (or being switched) to metered charging each year in England and Wales – a much higher figure than anything experienced in the recent past.

Australian utilities have employed a wide range of charging systems in the past, but (as noted in OECD, 1987a) once meters had been installed, the existing tariff structures generally provided very large free allowances which ensured that few customers actually entered the tranche where charging on the basis of consumption began. Recent reforms in Australia have quickened the pace of structural tariff reforms which were already in motion ten years ago. The result has been the virtual abolition of any free allowances – particularly the large ones. Only one of the smaller utilities maintains these allowances. A few utilities have also introduced increasing-block schedules. These changes serve social purposes, as well as generating powerful signals to encourage conservation. Although the first tranche is often available at a price well below long-run marginal costs where these volume-based systems operate, at least a non-zero price is now being attached to the demands that all households make upon the water systems.

Indeed, most water supply utility revenues in Australia are moving rapidly towards being based on actual usage, rather than on fixed charges. A decade ago, it was often the case that only about 20 per cent of water revenues came from usage charges. By 1996-97, utilities serving half of Australia's urban population were obtaining 65-80 per cent of their water revenues from volumetric charges. All other utilities (except for one, with a very large free allowance of 930 litres per household per day) were relying on volume charges for at least 50 per cent of their revenues. Six of the twelve utilities for which information was available for this study showed the "usage charge proportion" to have increased by between 10 per cent and 30 per cent over only a single year (1995-96 to 1996-97).

Charging traditions are also well-established in OECD Europe. **Luxembourg** has more than 100 communes which maintain a wide array of volumetric charging systems, some of them geared to social needs, with a sophistication probably unmatched anywhere else in the world. **Germany** and **Switzerland** both have long traditions of both "full cost recovery" and marginal cost pricing. Thus, recommendations have been made in Germany for the introduction of progressive tariff systems (increasing-block) to promote water economy objectives, and the possibility of the use of a purely quantity-based tariff (i.e. no fixed charge) has been discussed since at least 1990. This echoes the practice of some **Austrian** utilities. In this respect, it is interesting to note the continuing experience of Zurich, first highlighted in the 1987 study (Box 8 and Table 9).

Box 8.   Domestic Water Tariffs in Zurich, Switzerland

In the previous OECD study on water pricing (OECD, 1987a: Section III.4), attention was drawn to the unique situation of Zurich: the only water supply utility in Switzerland then administering an increasing-block tariff. In 1975, largely because of local groundwater pollution, the pricing system was radically altered to introduce an excess charge, to be applied only if a consumer had exceeded during the billing period a daily allocation geared to the size of the meter. Thus, a household is "allowed" to consume up to 1 000 litres/day at the "basic" price, and other customer classes were given higher specified allowances. For volumes consumed in excess of this limit, a significantly higher volumetric rate was charged, initially at double the basic price, but now believed to be about 40 per cent higher.

Together with important changes in wastewater tariffs in 1968 and 1971, this tariff restructuring was believed to be largely responsible for the reduction in overall consumption which took place between 1970 and 1984 (Table 9). Further reductions can be observed since 1984 as well. The addition of aggregate public water supply figures and estimates for the whole of Switzerland (in part, provided by SGWA) suggests that Zurich's tariff structure continues to exercise a significant influence on the water demands faced by the utility.

Table 9.   **Zurich PWS Usage and Estimates for Switzerland (1970-1997)**

	1970	1976	1984	1994	1997
Number of consumers in "excess tranche"		2 913 (7.3%)	1 770 (4.5%)		1 363 (3.7%)
Water consumption in excess (million m^3)		2.182 (3.4%)	0.704 (1.1%)		0.500 (0.9%)
Water consumption (million m^3) by:					
Normal users (0-9 999 m^3)	32.3	32.1	31.7		26.5
Large users (≥ 10 000 m^3)	18.4	16.4	15.9		12.7
Total consumption	50.7	48.5	47.6	41.0	39.2
Population of Switzerland (million)	6.0[1]		6.5	7.0	7.1[1]
Switzerland: PWS per capita (litres)	490		490	415	410[1]
Total PWS consumption (million m^3)	1 073[1]		1 163	1 063	1 063[1]

	Reduction in PWS consumption	
	1970-94[1]	1970-97[1]
Switzerland	1%	1%
Zurich	19%	23%

1.   Estimate only.
Source: OECD (1999c).

Wholly volumetric-based water tariff structures exist in both **Austria** and in some of the recent OECD countries (*e.g.* **Hungary, Poland,** and the **Czech Republic**). Discussion of a possible shift towards this type of "simplistic" volumetric pricing has recently been the subject of active debate in the **Netherlands** as well. Here, trials of the *Waterspoor* are being suggested to encourage more water saving.[9] This would involve the levying of water supply, sewerage, and water purification charges together, with both water supply and wastewater charges calculated on a volumetric basis. For water supply, the change would not be very significant, since the fixed element is only 5-10 per cent of the present metered bill. On the "dirty water" side, however, the impact of such a change would be considerable. Moving in a similar direction is the recent decision by both the Amsterdam and Rotterdam Water Boards (together with Antwerp, the last-remaining "big-city" outposts of unmeasured charging in continental Europe) to complete the individual metering of all households not resident in apartment blocks.

In **France** too, both the different components and the totality of the volumetric charge in consumer bills have been made more transparent as a result of an *arrêté* of July 1996, which lays down in considerable detail the legal content of a water bill. The demise (following the 1992 Water Law) of Type 3 tariffs in France (where the fixed charge "covers" a specified volume of household consumption per billing period), and the parallel increase in the use of Type 4 tariffs (fixed charge + a volumetric rate on all consumption), has led some observers to comment that high service fees ("as high as 90 per cent of water bills") can give municipal officials the scope to introduce tariff schedules with very low volumetric rates. These then "tend to work against the main goals of the 1992 Water Law", which seeks to avoid water waste and to promote equity between users (see Cambon-Grau and Barraqué, 1996). Even though Type 4 tariffs have the advantage that all water consumption attracts at least a positive marginal price, the most recent evidence suggests that the fixed elements in household bills are on average only 15 per cent (Conso 2000, 1996).

In 1994, a law was proposed in **Italy** for the total reorganisation of the Italian water industry. If implemented, this scheme would build up a single average cost-based volumetric price for the two main water services in each river catchment or "optimal management area" (OMA), with year-to-year price increases being capped by a complex formula involving assumed productivity growth potential, the inflation rate, and other factors. This average price would then be applied to the increasing-block tariff reforms which Italy has been using since the 1975 reforms. The basic principles of the block structure would remain unchanged, with a central block (tariff base) attracting the average cost based price and (as now) an initial subsidised block effectively financed by a number of more expensive blocks. The novel part of this scheme is that this increasing-block structure would be extended

to sewerage and sewage treatment, both of which are presently charged at constan:
volumetric rates. Thus, overall, the tariff structure for water services would become
significantly more progressive.

The prevailing tariff structure in **Greece** is motivated primarily by socia:
concerns; hence, there is a strong reliance on increasing-block tariff structure:
where volumetric charging is available. In addition, in order to address affordability
concerns, an upper bound on these tariffs is often applied for families with three or
more children. In Athens, the water supply tariff is made up of four elements:

- a fixed charge of GDR 480 /month;

- an increasing-block tariff;

- 8 per cent VAT; and

- an 18 per cent "tax" for "new projects and meter charges".

The crucial pricing step for the increasing-block tariff in place in Athens occurs
at about 20 m^3 of water per month per household (667 litres/day). At this point
access to cheap water stops (*i.e.* where households pay less than the price charged
to industry) and water becomes significantly more expensive (*i.e.* prices increase to
twice the levels paid by industry). Average *per capita* consumption by domestic users
in Athens is estimated to be 140 lhd so, allowing for scale economies in water use,
a household of five should therefore be able to stay in the cheap water tranche – at
least during climatically average periods of the year.

Municipalities in **Turkish** cities and urban areas also invariably operate
increasing-block tariffs for the household sector, with price increases tied to official
price indices. In **Spain** and in Lisbon (**Portugal**), conservation or social-based tariffs
(*i.e.* increasing-block) are also now dominant, usually with 3-5 blocks being used.
Barcelona in particular has pioneered the use of tariffs designed to combine strong
incentives to save water with a concern for social justice (Box 9).

As discussed above, time-of-day variations in tariff structures can be used to
smooth out water demand peaks, by shifting demands or removing them altogether. Although no examples of regular time-of-day variations in household water
tariffs were found in this study,[10] some US utilities were found to be using seasonal
tariffs. While a 1982 survey of nearly 100 US utilities found only one example of a
seasonal component in a residential public water supply tariff structure, a larger
survey in 1991 found seven utilities out of 121 had such a component (5.7 per cent
of the total). By 1997, this proportion had increased to ten utilities out of 121
(6.6 per cent) [Lippiatt and Weber (1982), Markus (1993), and Raftelis Environmental Consulting Group (1998)]. These figures suggest some expansion in the use of
seasonal tariffs during the 1980s, but the evidence also suggests this trend may
have slowed considerably during the 1990s.

Box 9. Household Water Tariffs in Barcelona, Spain

Catalonia has serious water pollution and water resource problems. In 1983, the Barcelona tariff system was therefore changed from a minimum-charge/ no-blocks/ no-fixed-charge structure to one with a fixed charge and just two blocks. During a drought in 1989, a third block was imposed, starting at 48 m³/quarter, and with a much higher price, in order to give the bigger domestic users a larger incentive to reduce their consumption. The present domestic tariff structure is illustrated below:

Band	Charge (Ptas/m³)	Proportion of domestic consumers in band(s)
0-18 m³/quarter	44.10	} 85% (0-48 m³)
18-48 m³/quarter	89.30	
> 48 m³/quarter	121.80	15%

Fixed charge per month *House type*	Charge (Ptas/month)
Type A	208
Types B and C	547
Types D and E	842
Types F	1 145

This structure has been refined in two important ways to enhance equity objectives. First, there is the variation in the fixed charge itself, which depends on the characteristics of the house. Second, for families with more than four people, the limit of the second block is now calculated by multiplying the number of people in the household by 11 m³. Thus the second block limits are:

Size of household	Second block (m³/quarter)
1-4 persons	18-48
5 persons	18-55
6 persons	18-66
7 persons	18-77
...	...

Virtually every household is metered (including all apartments individually), and the utility maintains that the tariff has been instrumental in reducing *per capita* household consumption from 211 lhd to 193 lhd between 1991 and 1996 (a reduction of 9 per cent).

61

In **Belgium,** the 1997 decision in the Region of Flanders to grant each house hold a free allowance in their water tariff geared to the number of people in the household (15 m³ of water per person per annum) breaks new ground for such a large area (about 6 million people). Until now, the main criticism of introducing a free- or low-price allowance has been that such allowances should optimally be associated with the *household*, rather than the *person*. The Flanders Region has now moved beyond that point by granting the allowance based on the number of occu-pants, a more equitable solution stemming from a desire to realise the resolution of the Rio Declaration (UN, 1992) which states a need for minimum access to fresh water of 40 litres per person per day. It is expected that this allowance is small enough to be both politically acceptable and not too distortive of pricing signals and structures.

However, preliminary results indicate that this initial free allowance may lead to some unexpected dynamic effects on prices and demand. Thus, since the intro-duction of the free allowance, the price of water has had to increase substantially (by about 40 per cent on average) in order to achieve the same level of cost recov-ery as before the free allowance (Nys, 1999). This may ultimately result in a substan-tial reduction in water usage (potentially with some consumers going "off tap"), which may again lead to price increases, generating a vicious circle of decreasing consumption and increasing unit costs (and prices) of water.

In Antwerp, there is also movement along these lines. The 1987 OECD study pointed out that Antwerp's unusual mixed (compulsory and optional) approach to metering domestic consumers – similar in some ways to the approach now being used in **England and Wales** – resulted in favouring unmetered consumption (*i.e.* 80:20). Ten years later, Antwerp water officials report that this balance had now swung to 70:30 – just the result which would be expected as increased incomes generate demand for more of the luxury water-using devices which disqualify con-sumers from retaining their unmetered status in the city.

In both **Japan** and **Korea,** as in other countries in the Asian region, most utilities use increasing-block tariff structures with a large number of blocks. In both coun-tries, the "basic rate" system – essentially, a minimum consumption charge which usually covers the first 10 m³/month for each household – has been applied as a fixed charge base, on which the rest of the tariff structure is then constructed.

There have been recent debates about the basic rate's future in both of these countries. Faced with the fact that water prices were raising revenues equal to only 77 per cent of the total cost of water provision for **Korea** as a whole, the government issued in 1996 the *Comprehensive Water Management Countermeasures*. Following this, 59 of the 167 local governments in the country abandoned the basic rate and raised the price of water. The official reason given at the time for abandoning minimum consumption charging was to persuade people to be more careful in their use of water.

Finally, an interesting development has recently occurred in **Ireland.** In 1978, domestic rates were abolished in that country, and water charges also disappeared. However, in 1983, the *possibility* of separate charges was re-introduced for a number of local services, including water, with local authorities having discretion in the matter. By 1996, domestic water supply charges existed in 86 of 88 local authorities – all except Dublin and Limerick. Wastewater charges were also being levied by 31 local authorities. In 1996, however, the government decided to consolidate domestic water charges entirely into the general taxation system. This change took effect on 1 January 1997, and has since been the subject of considerable debate.

Industrial tariff structures

On average, less than one-quarter of industrial water used in OECD countries is drawn from the public water supply system. By far the majority of water consumed for industrial purposes is abstracted directly by industrial users, for reasons discussed below. The discussion in this section therefore refers only to that (small) percentage of industrial water that is drawn from the public system.

Few hard and fast rules can be discerned about industrial water tariff policies across the OECD Region, largely due to the diversity encountered within the countries themselves. Industrial users are sometimes charged according to a similar tariff structure as domestic users, and sometimes this structure is very different. Thus, domestic users are charged on the basis of flat rates in a number of countries, while industrial users are almost always metered. In **Iceland,** for example, domestic users pay an annual fixed charge per m^2 of property, plus an overall charge per property, whereas industrial users are billed according to a two-part tariff, with the fixed charge varying according to the meter size.

Table 10 provides an overview of the existing situation in OECD countries in terms of the charges levied on industrial water consumers using the public water supply system.

Price structures for industrial consumers are generally fixed at the local (municipal) level, and can vary widely within a country (*e.g.* in order to reflect differences in cost structures). The most common structures are two-part tariffs, including a fixed element, which generally varies according to some characteristic of the user, and a variable element, usually based on average cost pricing. The fixed element can be based on the meter size (as in **Portugal,** and generally in **Australia**), on pipe size (as in **Japan** and **Korea**), or on property value (as in some cases in **Australia,** although these are gradually being phased out), in order to account for the capacity requested by the industrial customer (*i.e.* its contribution to peak demand). In some countries, the fixed element is simply presented as a meter fee (*e.g.* **Iceland, Italy,** and **Turkey**).

OECD 1999

Table 10. **Price Structure for Industrial Water Services From the Public System**

	Tariff structure	FCR	ND	MC	DTS	Special tariffs	Subsidies
Australia	Fixed + volume-based	Yes	No	Yes	Yes	No	n.a.
Austria	Fixed + volume-based	Yes	No	n.a.	No	n.a.	Yes
Belgium	Fixed (meter rental) + volume-based	Yes	Yes	n.a.	No	Large volumes	Regional
Canada	Flat rates (annual fees) or volume-based, decreasing-blocks	No	No	No	Yes	Contract-based	Yes
Czech Republic	n.a.	Yes	No	n.a.	Yes	Contract-based (lower quality)	Yes
Denmark	Connection (based on area) + fixed (various bases) + volume-based	Yes	Yes	n.a.	No	No	No
Finland	Connection + fixed (meter and property size) + volume	Yes	Yes	No	No	Exceptionally contract-based (large users)	Negligible
France	Connection + fixed + volume (decreasing-blocks)	Yes	Yes	Yes	Yes	Contract-based	Yes
Germany	Fixed + volume-based	Yes	Yes	Yes	Yes	Large users, contract-based	No
Greece	Connection + volume-based	n.a.	No	n.a.	Yes	n.a.	Yes
Hungary	Volume-based	n.a.	n.a.	n.a.	n.a.	Capital contributions	Yes
Iceland	Fixed (meter fee) + volume (varies with meter size)	n.a.	n.a.	n.a.	Yes	n.a.	n.a.
Ireland	Connection + volume-based	No	No	n.a.	Yes	Capital contributions	Yes
Italy	Fixed (meter fee) + volume-based (rising blocks)	No	No	Yes	No	Industrial networks	Yes
Japan	Fixed (pipe size) + volume	No	No	No	n.a.	Contract-based	Yes
Korea	Fixed (pipe size) + volume	Yes	No	No	No	No	Yes
Mexico	Fixed + volume (majority are increasing-block tariffs)	No	No	No	n.a.	n.a.	Yes
Netherlands	Connection + fixed (size of meter) + volume-based	Yes	Yes	No	No	Operating hours	No
New Zealand	Annual fee + volume-based	n.a.	n.a.	n.a.	n.a.	n.a.	n.a.
Norway	Connection + fixed charge	Yes	n.a.	n.a.	n.a.	n.a.	Regional
Poland	Volume-based charge	n.a.	No	n.a.	n.a.	n.a.	Yes
Portugal	Fixed (meter size) + volume (increasing-blocks)	No	n.a.	Yes	n.a.	n.a.	n.a.
Spain	Diversity of structures; majority are increasing (two-blocks)	No	n.a.	n.a.	n.a.	n.a.	Yes
Sweden	Fixed (size of industrial estate, meter size) + volume-based	Yes	No	No	No	Cooling water tariff, no seasonal.	No

OECD 1999

Table 10. **Price Structure for Industrial Water Services From the Public System** *(cont.)*

	Tariff structure	FCR	ND	MC	DTS	Special tariffs	Subsidies
Switzerland	Fixed + volume-based	n.a.	n.a.	n.a.	n.a.	n.a.	n.a.
Turkey	Fixed + volume-based	No	No	No	Yes	Contracts	n.a.
UK	Connection + Fixed (pipe size) + volume-based	Yes	Yes	No	Yes	Large-user tariffs	No
US	Connection and development fees; diversity of block structures, but most are increasing-block rates	Yes	No	No	Yes	Seasonal tariffs; excess use charges	No

n.a. Not available.
Notes:
Tariff structure: What are the types of *tariff structures* in place?
FCR: Is there *full cost recovery*? (*i.e.* are total revenues required to cover operating expenditure, plus depreciation, plus a return on capital employed?)
ND: Is *non-discrimination* a requirement? (*i.e.* are the tariffs for each customer group required to reflect the costs of the customer group concerned?)
MC: Is there any *marginal cost pricing*?
DTS: Do industrial customers have a *different tariff structure* to other customers?
Special tariffs: Are there any *special tariffs* for industrial customers?
Subsidies: Are there any *subsidies*?

OECD 1999

In addition, a connection charge may be levied separately, as in **Denmark,** **Finland, France, Greece, Ireland, Netherlands, Norway, UK** and the **US**. The basis for defining the connection charge can vary substantially. In **Denmark**, for instance, industrial users pay a charge based on a unit area of 800 m² of property.

Another type of charge which is specifically applied to industrial users is a capital contribution for special investment works. These can be seen as a form of "full cost recovery" pricing, since the relevant share of investment costs would be covered by industrial users in this case. In **Hungary** and **Ireland**, for example, some waterworks have introduced capital charges on users to cover new investments, as a "one-off" charge.

Little information is available on tariff structures for industrial consumers in some countries, because industrial users often tend to enter into special contracts with water suppliers. Such contract-based tariffs are found, for example, in **Canada**, the **Czech Republic, France, Germany** (usually in the industrialised northern part of the country), and **Japan**. Contract terms are generally not made public and no statistics are available. Sometimes, these contracts can involve the supply of lower-quality water (which would be unsuitable for domestic water use), as in the **Czech Republic.**

Special tariff arrangements are also sometimes available for an entire class of industrial customers, rather than being based on bilateral negotiations. In the **UK**, for example, "large user" tariffs were introduced in England and Wales in 1993. At the time, the economic regulator (the Director-General of Water Services) was asked to determine whether these special tariffs conformed to the requirement of avoiding "undue discrimination and preference" that had been imposed on water companies in their licences. The reasons given by the regulator at the time to justify discounts for industrial users included: "... large users may have more stable demands, avoid some peak costs (particularly if on-site storage is provided). Where water is supplied in large pipes, some of the costs in the distribution system (including leakage) may also be avoided" (Ofwat, 1993). Where these factors are relevant enough, the regulator specified that they had no opposition to them being reflected in the tariffs, though preferably through standard charges available to all customers in similar circumstances, rather than by special agreement.

The rationale that lower tariffs may be available on the grounds that industrial users simply consume larger volumes was specifically rejected by the UK regulator, but is applied in **Belgium**. There, the largest consumers can negotiate special supply contracts with distribution companies, on the basis of which prices can be reduced to half the value of normal prices.

Similarly, decreasing-block tariffs (where successive blocks of water are sold at lower and lower prices) are present in some regions of the **US**. This is especially the case in industrialised regions with a lot of heavy industry (*e.g.* the Great Lakes), where they are seen as an instrument to favour industrial users. While these used to be very common in the US, they are now slowly disappearing (and have even been banned in Massachusetts).

Increasing-block tariffs for industrial water use (which encourage water conservation practices) exist in **Italy, Portugal, Spain,** and the **US.** In **Spain,** there is a large diversity of tariff structures, but most involve increasing two-block tariffs. In the US, increasing-block tariffs are now favoured more often, especially in the West, where conservation objectives are prevalent because of repeated drought conditions. In Los Angeles, for instance, a seasonal increasing-block rate structure has recently been adopted, with rates being adjusted for "average prior use" by industrial users.

While such seasonal tariffs for industrial water use are in place in some parts of the **US,** they are still not very common in Europe. They exist in some **French** municipalities, but are explicitly banned in **Sweden.** Seasonal tariffs are one favoured way of introducing marginal cost pricing elements in the tariff structure.

As mentioned above, flat rate tariffs are rare for industrial users, because these users are almost always metered, and most revenue is collected on a volumetric basis. In **Canada,** however, industrial water tariff structures are rarely based on economic principles, and some flat rates have been used. In particular, industrial firms can negotiate contracts with municipalities for water services, and these contracts are normally negotiated at bulk rates, unrelated to the precise quantities of water used.

Agricultural tariff structures

As with industrial and household water demands, agricultural water usage is far from homogeneous, even within individual countries. Marginal cost charging is rarely encountered in irrigation water prices. More commonly, irrigation prices are intended only to make farmers responsible for the variable costs of supplying water, whereas part or all the fixed costs are covered by public agencies, at taxpayers' cost. In many cases, an individual farmer's water consumption is not metered, so the range of available pricing mechanisms is more limited.

In addition to the standard volumetric and fixed tariffs, agricultural water pricing tariffs in at least some OECD countries also reflect the following structures (adapted from Tsur and Dinar, 1997):

- *Area-pricing*: charges for water used per unit of irrigated area. Sometimes area-pricing discriminates based on either the crops irrigated, the irrigation technologies used, or the season of the year.

- *Tiered-pricing* (sometimes called "block-rate" pricing): different prices for the volumes of water expected to be used in different ways.

67

- *Betterment levy-pricing*: charges irrigated land based on the increased value of land, due to the provision of irrigation water.
- *Water markets* (including auctions): public agencies can elicit farmers' "willingness-to-pay" for marginal units of water, and set prices accordingly.
- *Passive trading* (as suggested by Brill *et al.* (1997): the district offers a price – presumably the one which equates aggregate water supply and demand – and farmers make use of whatever amount of water they want. Farmers' consolidated rights to water are then charged at the average price, but those whose consumption is higher would have to pay the offered price, and those consuming below their rights would receive a payment for their thrift.
- *Volumetric pricing (of any kind), with a bonus*: farmers are required to pay for any water that exceeds a certain volume, and are financially rewarded if their consumption is below another threshold.

In view of the very diverse water resource situations which exist, drawing comparisons of pricing structures across OECD countries is a complex task. In addition to the conceptual vagueness created by the use of common words to denote different things ("full cost recovery" being perhaps the best example), cross-country comparisons will ultimately be based on general trends which mask important deviations within individual countries. Nevertheless, some generic factors do seem to contribute to at least a partial explanation of the observed differences in agricultural pricing structures in the OECD Region.

Roughly speaking, OECD countries can be divided into three main groups, according to the role played by, and the potential productivity of, irrigated farming. One group comprises those countries/regions which have climates that make irrigated agriculture much more productive than dry-land agriculture. This group includes **Australia, Greece, Spain, Western US, Mexico, Portugal, Turkey, Japan,** and **Southern Italy.** The second group includes those countries/regions in which irrigation is carried out mainly as a complement to climate conditions which are otherwise favourable to dry-land agriculture. This group includes **Northern France, Northern Italy, New Zealand, Canada,** and the **UK (England and Wales).** These are countries/regions in which irrigated agriculture is still increasing, and where farmers are still investing in irrigation equipment, but primarily in order to reduce risk. The third group includes countries/regions in which irrigated agriculture is negligible, or where it is generally limited to horticultural productions in the summer time. The countries in this group are **Norway, Austria, Sweden, Finland, Denmark, Netherlands, Belgium, Poland, Czech Republic, Germany,** and **Switzerland.**

The first group is certainly the most complex and heterogeneous (Table 11). Some of the common features of this group include strong inter-sectoral competition for water resources; wide differences in net agricultural returns, depending on whether or not irrigation exists; long and deep involvement of public

Table 11. Agricultural Water Pricing Structures in Selected OECD Countries

	Types of water rights		Pricing criteria/Agency	Recovered costs	Differential charges based on:				Other factors		Performance	Other economic instruments	Inter-sector water competition	On-going reforms
	Surface	Ground-water			EQ	LQ	HR	IT	ATP	AP				
Australia	Entitlements	Licensed	Federal Guidelines and State (or other jurisdiction) criteria	O&M + salinity control and capital replacement	No	No	Yes	No	Initially	No	Good	Tradable permits; caps on diversions	Strong	Full cost recovery expected to be completed by 2001
Belgium (Flanders)	Use rights	Geographically and historically defined	Prices set by individual distribution companies, within provincial jurisdiction. Federal government controls prices	100% of costs for piped water; levy on declared quantities of surface and groundwater abstractions	No	No	Yes	No	No	No	Good	Pollution charges	Light	n.a.
Canada	Use permits	Free (provincial variations)	Provincial level and water agencies	O&M	No	No	No	No	Yes	No	Poor	Tradable permits (Alberta); environmental regulations	Light	Budgetary constraints; stringent environmental regulations
France	Use rights	n.a.	Regional Development Companies	O&M + capital replacement	Yes	No	No	Yes	Yes	No	Fair	Quotas (depending on water availability)	Climate-dependent	General trend towards use of pricing, but subsidies to irrigation equipment also induce the expansion of irrigation
Germany	Use rights	n.a.	Länder	Extraction costs	n.a.	n.a.	n.a.	n.a.	n.a.	n.a.	Poor	Tax-exemptions for farmers	Light	Stringent environmental regulations
Greece	Use rights	Licence	Regional Devt Agreements and private suppliers	O&M + administration costs	Yes	Yes	No	Yes	Yes	Yes	Poor	Agricultural policies; rural development policies	Strong	National Land Registry; creation of self-financed Water Management Agencies
Italy	License	License	Irrigation boards	O&M (+ % of capital replacement)	No	No	No	Yes	No	No	Poor	Quotas; progressive pricing in the South	Strong in the South	Devolution of public systems to local governments; integrated water management plans
Japan	Historical and use rights to WUAs	Not used	Districts	O&M (+ % of capital replacement)	Yes	Yes	Yes	No	Yes	Yes	Fair	Agric. struct. reforms; transferability (in-kind)	Strong (during droughts)	Districts' rehabilitation programs; modest liberalisation; consistency with agricultural policies
Mexico	Use rights (50 years)	n.a.	Federal level and irrigation "modules"	O&M	Yes	Yes	No	No	Yes	Yes	Fair	Agric. policies; water planning	Strong	Decentralisation; devolution toward irrigation "modules"; rehabilitation projects

OECD 1999

Table 11. **Agricultural Water Pricing Structures in Selected OECD Countries** *(cont.)*

	Types of water rights		Pricing criteria/Agency	Recovered costs	Differential charges based on:				Other factors		Performance	Other economic instruments	Inter-sector water competition	On-going reforms
	Surface	Ground-water			EQ	LQ	HR	IT	ATP	AP				
Netherlands	Use rights	License	Water Control Boards (cost-based, including treatment)	O&M	No	No	n.a.	No	No	No	Good	Pollution and flood control levies	Low	Moving towards a different view of flood security policies
New Zealand	Use rights (resource consents)	Use rights (resource consents)	Local authorities and irrigation schemes	100% of costs	No	No	No	No	No	No	Good	No	Increasing	Increased water metering; price differentials, depending on farmers' costs
Portugal	Public and private rights	n.a.	Government and private water company criteria	O&M	Yes	Yes	Yes	Yes	Yes	Yes	Poor	Agric. policies; rural development	Low	Alqueva project will set the new water pricing policy, but it is still largely undefined
Spain	Use rights	Licenses (but almost private)	River Basin Agencies (by law) and Irrigation Districts	O&M (+ % of capital replacement)	Yes	Yes	Yes	Yes	No	Yes	Poor	Quotas (allotments); occasional markets	Strong	Items under discussion include: an amendment to the Water Law; a national water management plan; and a national irrigation plan
Turkey	Use rights	Licenses	National Government and WUAs	O&M	Yes	Yes	No	Yes	Yes	Yes	Poor	Agric. Policy	Low	Transfer of O&M cost collection responsibility to WUAs
UK	Licenses	Licences	National River Agencies and Water Companies	100%	No	No	No	Yes	No	No	Fair	Quotas	Increasing in some areas	Wider metering of water consumption; possible implementation of incentive charges and permit trading
US	Private and public rights	Private	Federal and State Agencies	O&M (+ % of capital in California)	No	No	Yes	No	Yes	No	Fair	Tradeability; water banks (in-kind exchanges)	Strong	Stringent environmental requirements; block-rate prices; devolution to WUAs

n.a. Not available.
Notes:
– EQ: equity considerations (are prices adjusted in order to avoid wide differences among irrigators?)
– LQ: Do land quality considerations justify different price levels?
– HR: Do historical rights explain any price variations (holding other factors constant)?
– IT: Is irrigation technology taken into account when setting charges?
– ATP: "Ability-to-pay".
– AP: Is general agricultural policy taken into account when setting charges.
– Performance is rated by comparing the objectives of each country's charging systems with their accomplishments.

agencies in building water works and/or irrigation projects; increasing difficulties in preserving the environmental quality of waterways, without reducing the quantity available to users; and increasing costs of generating new sources of water supply.

Despite these similarities, these countries do differ in the relative "maturity" of their agricultural water economies. The most mature are perhaps **Australia, Spain, US,** and **Japan.** These countries experienced 10-20 years ago the same types of expansion that **Portugal, Greece, Mexico,** or **Turkey** are undergoing at the moment. In **Portugal** and **Turkey,** in particular, large-scale expansion of irrigated land is still possible, and is in fact a general public policy objective. In Turkey, for example, it is estimated that less than one-third of available surface waters, and only about half of the available annually-recharged groundwater resources, are currently being utilised. Approximately 8.5 million hectares is considered to be economically-irrigable, using current technology. Slightly less than half of this area is being irrigated at the moment.

As noted earlier, there has been a significant recent trend in Turkey toward the transfer of irrigation schemes out of state control, and into the control of local users. Agricultural water prices in Turkey are, in principle, set with the recovery of operating costs in mind. Water rates are imposed on the basis of the amount of cropped-area (and thus are not charged in proportion with actual consumption), with different rates being charged for different crops, to reflect differences in water requirements for each crop. The main future challenges to the Turkish water economy are likely to be: *i*) environmental issues, such as salinity build-up and erosion); and *ii*) urban encroachment on agricultural land

Japan's case is not matched by any of the other countries surveyed in this report. Japan is perhaps the country whose agricultural water economy has the strongest ties to tradition and history, and whose agricultural sector is the most structured. Flat rates are generally levied, which, under most circumstances, would provide disincentives to use water efficiently. However, this has not been the case in Japan (Box 10). In general, there is little political support for any policy changes that would worsen the financial situation of paddy growers – and volumetric water pricing is perceived as one such change. Japan now seems inclined to modestly liberalise the allocation of water rights, thus drawing some advantages from the increasing willingness of urban suppliers to pay for water, and contributing new revenues for rehabilitating the older, and very "atomised" water districts. Clearly, this approach is not aimed at reversing a situation which has existed for centuries, but at attracting non-rural capital in order to persuade water rights holders to accept "in-kind" water trading, without encroaching upon their traditional rights or vested positions. It can therefore be argued that, so long as all stakeholders agree on the criteria used in sharing available resources, it may be possible to achieve efficient water use and allocation, without either metering it, or applying incentive-based rates for its use.

Box 10. Efficiency Without Incentive-based Pricing

Despite the use of non-volumetric water tariff structures, the *Japanese* agricultural sector succeeds in effectively managing its irrigation water demands. Three factors in particular help to alleviate the presumed efficiency losses of flat rate pricing, and indicate a considerable ability by the irrigation districts to ration water under stressful conditions (Nakashima, 1997). First, most farmers grow rice and have very similar types of land-holdings. Second, anecdotal evidence seems to indicate that farmers use water at marginal productivities greater than zero, due to self-restraint in water abstractions, and in order to avoid both regional disputes and the environmental deterioration of rivers. Third, although water prices *themselves* are flat, farmers do incur additional marginal costs in *using* that water, which might induce them to increase marginal productivities. In fact, under stressful drought conditions, water application costs usually increase sharply, because water has to be managed very closely, thereby rationing its use at farm levels.

This reasoning is also applied to the most traditional irrigated areas of **Spain**, where the institutional framework has shown remarkable adaptability to natural variations in water supplies for centuries. Especially at the district or retail level, farmers' associations have shown remarkable ability to raise enough revenues to cover the their own costs of allocating water under stressful conditions, to maintain and improve their assets, to solve internal conflicts, and to find ways of enlarging their water resource base, mostly through private investments. Overall, these co-operatively run institutions, some of which are several centuries old, suggest that efficient allocations of scarce water resources can sometimes occur *without* incentive-based pricing structures.

The **Greek** water economy is also quite heterogeneous and, with 20 per cent of the active population making its living from agriculture, is subject to both general agricultural and rural development policies. At the moment, the top priorities of the government are: *i)* the completion of a National Land Registry that will permit the authorities to have more effective control over water and land uses; *ii)* improvements in the water rights allocation process, so that all users will eventually have water rights (as envisaged under current legislation); and *iii)* constructing ambitious water facilities to attenuate the effects of droughts to provide guaranteed access to water resources in tourist areas. In these contexts, pricing policies are only seen to be important where they contribute to infrastructure rehabilitation projects in industrial districts, or in cities.

The Capitanata region of **Southern Italy** provides another example which differs from the experience of other countries. In Capitanata, water is a scarce, but agriculturally-productive, resource. Irrigation districts are given considerable power to allot water quotas, to charge prices that generate enough revenue to cover O&M expenses, and to discourage excessive water application rates. A new programme there encourages improved management of the collective irrigation system and wastewater recovery, as well as introducing a two-part charging system that discourages water use levels which exceed crops' critical water needs. Water scarcities and the considerable institutional authority of district water managers explains much of the successful experience with water pricing which has been observed.

Among the countries belonging to Group 1, **Australia** has gone the furthest in reforming its agricultural water pricing arrangements. Some of the most important structural aspects of these reforms have included:

- Further abstractions in over-appropriated basins were capped. Water could no longer be made available to any applicant who wanted access to the resource. In general, environmental quality enhancement became one of the government's top priorities.

- The new pricing criteria could not discriminate among farmers, land quality, or any other factor. Prices would henceforth be set in line with estimated water supply costs. The estimation procedure was designed at Federal level, following lengthy negotiations, and was set in such a way that each water user or sector should cover the costs it generated on its own.

- The procedures used to estimate water service costs should be respected by individual States, so that price distortions across borders would not exist.

- Water entitlements were converted into tradable property rights. Those farmers who do not generate enough net returns to pay the new water prices are allowed to sell their entitlements. Because of the difficulties of implementing such a system, trading of water entitlements is being introduced progressively.

Mexico's situation differs from Australia's in that its general economic reforms have lagged behind reforms in the water sector. The main force leading the reform here has been the steady decline in the quality of irrigation facilities, which had the effect of rendering huge areas of irrigated land virtually useless. This was the result of a failure to raise enough revenue to match O&M costs, with farmers' contributions accounting for only 37 per cent of these costs by 1990 – down from 95 per cent in 1950 (Johnson, 1997). This was exacerbated by the 1982 economic crisis, which put an end to decades of government investment in irrigation projects and water harnessing facilities.

Mexico's pricing reforms seek to improve the management of water at the irrigation district level, and to make wholesale and retail water allocation systems less vulnerable to cyclical shortfalls in federal budgets. Large irrigation units, which had proven too big to be adequately managed, were broken up into smaller districts, and given more administrative independence to collect charges on their own, to maintain collective assets, and to manage their water resources. These reforms have managed to partially equip many irrigation districts with the tools needed to guarantee that farmers' charges are sufficient to sustainably maintain the operational capacity of their assets. These "modules" are now operating at 80 per cent of financial self-sufficiency (in terms of operating and maintenance costs).

The **Spanish** case is both complex and extremely diverse in terms of performance and pricing criteria. Water use rights here are solidly connected to land use rights, and water markets are therefore not permitted. Although water is structurally and/or cyclically scarce in large parts of the country, public pricing policies are not used to ration access to these resources. The Water Law sets clear guidelines as to what charges can be imposed on farmers using surface waters. In spite of these guidelines, however, agricultural water charges have not matched the O&M expenses of basin agencies, nor has that portion of capital costs which should be legally assigned to irrigators been recovered.

At the wholesale level, both public policies and the institutional framework in place in Spain exhibit a tendency to continue to expand, even though it seems clear that Spain reached "infrastructure maturity" some time ago. Indicators of this further expansion include: i) irrigation districts are still being built with subsidies, and total abstractions are still increasing in basins which are prone to drought conditions; ii) irrigation water is far from being considered a valuable economic commodity; iii) collection of charges is not universal; and iv) most water "bottlenecks" are being tackled by building new structural facilities, rather than by increasing prices. In general, attempts to implement more ambitious water pricing systems are being hindered by several factors:

– new irrigation districts are still being built at subsidised costs;

– agricultural water demand at zero or very low prices is still being met by subsidised structural facilities – although this practice is now becoming less wide-spread; and

– the Water Law currently in force severely restricts the ability of basin agencies to increase water charges.

The **Western US** agricultural water economy is even more complex. Although the Federal Bureau of Reclamation (BoR) has played a leading role in expanding irrigated land in this region, the States have considerable authority to pursue quite different approaches to water pricing, to promote (or to refrain from) further irrigation projects, and to set their individual water-related priorities. Broadly, two priorities drive public water policy development here. One is to find ways of meeting the increasing demands of most Western cities, and to improve the reliability of this supply. The other is to enhance the environmental conditions of rivers and lakes, to protect wildlife, and to preserve natural habitats. Irrigators therefore find themselves in the middle of most water disputes, and access to their water rights is often viewed as a viable solution for alleviating any water scarcities that may be identified.

Most US analysts seem to concur that the option of increasing water prices is overrated. Several reasons have been put forward against making wider use of public pricing mechanisms (OECD, 1999b). As in other OECD countries, one of these is that increasing prices would penalise farmers who bought land at prices in which access to subsidised water had already being capitalised. Another reason is that farmers' water rights are solidly entrenched in the legal system, so any attempt to charge farmers a higher price could be easily challenged on legal grounds. The final reason is that water pricing would be inefficient, in view of the general lack of information facing water management agencies.

California's 1991 Central Valley Project provides a different example. Although tiered water-pricing has been implemented for farm use of water from this project, contract renewals are taking place at a very slow pace, because most farmers still have long-term contracts with the BoR.

In sum, the implementation of irrigation water pricing seems to be out of the question in most US States. Instead, some regions (e.g. Western US) are attempting to exploit other types of market or incentive mechanisms, such as water banks or "in-kind" water trading arrangements, in order to provide appropriate signals about water scarcities.

The second group of countries noted earlier consists of those in which irrigation is still expanding. However, each country's institutional framework again follows somewhat different paths. At one extreme, **New Zealand's** irrigated land expansion has resulted from private entrepreneurs seeking profits by servicing irrigation water to farmers, or by groups of farmers who associate in order to build collective private facilities. As part of the major economic reforms which took place in that country in the late 1980s, the government was able to sell all its irrigation projects, putting an end to public involvement in irrigated agriculture. New Zealand's public policy has thus been limited to granting "resource consents" to applicants, and to charging permit holders with adequate prices to cover all administrative costs. Other water service costs, at both wholesale and retail levels, are paid by final users.

In the **UK,** the pricing institutions are similar to those which exist in New Zealand, with extraction licenses (with concomitant extraction fees) being restricted by an overall quota. Each region has been allowed since 1993 to set charges in line with its specific water control costs and variability. While there has been some installation of on-farm water meters, in general water management is based primarily on levying flat fees or the use of quotas and licenses to restrict water use.

75

Agricultural water pricing policies in **France, Northern Italy,** and **Canada** are also evolving towards full cost recovery, although each country is following a somewhat different path in implementing these reforms. In **France,** pricing policies are being combined with other instruments (such as water allocations and quotas), and are designed by the regional agencies responsible for managing water resources at the wholesale level. In this sense, the French system grants each of the River Basin Agencies broad independence to design and implement local water policies, which generally seem quite well-suited to the hydrologic conditions prevailing in each area.

In **Northern Italy** and **Canada,** agricultural water institutions do not suffer the periodically stressful conditions that exist in some parts of France. A key motivation for both countries to charge higher water prices to farmers is simply that new sources of revenue are needed to pay for water supply. Thus, the Italian government has recently reduced the level of subsidies to water supply facilities, although farmers still pay much less than other water users. Similarly, tighter federal budgets, together with the inability to raise enough revenue, have prompted many Canadian agencies to implement new agricultural water pricing policies. The Province of Alberta has perhaps made the greatest progress towards water pricing liberalisation, justified by the water scarcity problems that are occasionally experienced there. Alberta's 1996 Water Act is unique within Canada, in that water rights trading has been given a key role in efforts to obtain efficiency gains, whereas the other provinces are relying entirely on public pricing approaches (Horbulyk and Lo, 1998).

The third group of countries is characterised by farmers having easy access to water resources, and by the fact that aggregate consumption is not very significant, relative to total abstractions. Agricultural water pricing policies in all of these countries are much less important *per se* than the other policies which affect irrigation and non-irrigation farming, including general natural resources management policies. In these countries, water pricing policies are therefore virtually non-existent.

5.2. Tariff levels

Household tariff levels

Use of taxes and charges

Table 12 illustrates that there is a broad range of practices in the OECD concerning the imposition of water taxes and charges on piped household services (*i.e.* in addition to the base water charges). VAT is the most common type of tax. Within OECD Europe, **Finland, Sweden, Norway,** and **Denmark** all charge VAT on

Table 12. **Taxes and Levies in Household Water Tariffs**[1]

Per cent

	Public water supply		
	VAT	Abstraction charge	Other taxes
Australia		–	
Austria	10	–	
Belgium	6	v	
Czech Republic	5		
Denmark	25	–	v[2]
Finland	22	–	–
France	5.5	v	v[3]
Germany	7	v[4]	v[4]
Greece			8[5]
Hungary	12	v	–
Ireland	Domestic water charges consolidated into general taxation		
Italy	9	v	
Japan	5[6]	v	
Korea	–	–	–
Luxembourg		–	
Mexico		v	
Netherlands	6	v[7]	
Norway	22		
Poland		v	
Portugal	5	–[8]	
Spain	6	v	
Sweden	25	–[9]	–[9]
Switzerland	0	–	
Turkey	15	–	
UK:	0		
Eng and Wales		v	–
N. Ireland		–	–
Scotland		–	–

Notes: A "blank" cell implies that data were not available; a cell with a "–" indicates "no charge"; and a cell with a "v" indicates that a charge is actually levied.

1. This Table lists taxes and other charges included or reflected in the water bills of domestic consumers. It lists charges levied in addition to "regular" piped water supply.
2. Water levy per m[3].
3. FNDAE tax is raised to subsidise rural water systems.
4. Abstraction charges are 0-0.6 DM per m[3]. There are also administrative fees associated with water abstraction which can amount to a few per cent of the water bill.
5. An 8% tax is imposed on the price of water. There is also an 18% charge for "new projects and meter charges", but the precise status of this charge is unclear.
6. 5% consumption tax.
7. Tax on groundwater abstractions only (which represents 60% of PWS, however).
8. Planned.
9. Currently under formal discussion.

water services at more than 20 per cent. At the other extreme, the **UK** "zero-rates" water services, while the remaining **EU** members have rates between 5 per cent and 10 per cent for piped water supplies. The **Netherlands** has recently accepted a

77

law that will raise the VAT applied to domestic water consumption in 1999, from the low tariff (6 per cent) to the high one (17.5 per cent) for all water use exceeding 60 guilders per annum per household. In the context of "greening" the tax system, only the first 60 guilders worth is considered "essential", with consumption above this level considered a "luxury".

Other distinctive taxes on water use are found in **France** and **Denmark**, and are currently under discussion in **Sweden**. In France, the tax levied for the *Fonds National Des Adductions d'Eau* (FNDAE) adds about 1 per cent to water bills, and provides funds to the supply of rural water and wastewater services (effectively financing some of the capital costs). It is essentially a cross-subsidy between groups of water users (*i.e.* from non-rural to rural consumers), but is still consistent with the idea of "full cost recovery" across all water services and all consumers.

In **Denmark**, the water tax of 1 DKr/m^3 introduced in 1994 was increased to its target level of 5 DKr/m^3 in 1998. In **Sweden**, there is discussion about the possibility of a new tax on water use and/or discharges. The government recently proposed (spring 1998) that a parliamentary committee develop such a system.

Water tariffs

Table 13 illustrates (in a common form, and on a common basis) average measures of household water charges in OECD countries, using the most recent information available. For this exercise, two different types of data have been used: first, the cost of a country's average or typical household bill (for example, by selecting a "typical" annual consumption rate); second, the addition of the average of different utilities' fixed charge elements to the average of their volumetric rates, transforming the former into a "volumetric-equivalent" rate by assuming a typical household consumption rate.

These calculations are undertaken in national currencies, separately for PWS and wastewater where possible (wastewater pricing practices are discussed in Chapter 7), and for both of them combined, with account being taken of the relative importance of the fixed charge element in all three cases. The final column in the first part of Table 13 transforms the local currency (combined) volumetric rates into US$ equivalents, using average market exchange rates for the relevant year, in order to facilitate comparisons. Note, however, that the usefulness of such an exercise is quite limited. Strictly speaking, the only comparison it permits is from the point of view of a household unit with given financial resources (in US$) comparing the prices of an "average" bundle of water services in different countries, with the average itself varying across countries.

In the first part of Table 13, it can be seen that the fixed (*i.e.* non-volumetric) shares of average PWS bills lie between zero (for **Austria**, the **Czech Republic**, and **Hungary**) and 49 per cent (for **Japan**). For wastewater services, the fixed share varies

Table 13. **Household Tariffs: Levels and Recent Trends**

	Year	Water service prices per m³ (fixed element as % of total, in brackets)						Recent % increase		
		Currency	Measure	PWS	S&ST	Total	US$	Year / Measure	Nominal	Real p.a.
Australia	1996-97	A$	AV-68%	0.95 (36%)	1.11 (96%)	2.06 (69%)	1.64	1995-96 AV	0.7	-0.6
Austria	1997	AS	WAV	12.9 (0%)	n.a.		1.05	n.a.		
Belgium:								1988-98 ("COW")	65	2.7
Flanders	1997	FB	B (120), AV	60.0 (16%)	24.5 (0%)	84.5 (10%)	2.36			
Brussels	1997	FB	B (120), AV	59.6 (11%)	14 (0%)	73.6 (9%)	2.06			
Wallonia	1997	FB	B (120), AV	60.5 (13%)	16 (0%)	76.5 (10%)	2.14			
Canada	1994	CAN$	AB (300)	n.a.	n.a.	1.03 (44%)	0.70	1986-96 AB-PWS	73	2.9
Czech Republic	1997	KCS	AV	12.2(0%)	9.4 (0%)	21.6 (0%)	(0.68)	1990-97 AV	2 591	n.a.
Denmark	1995	DKR	B (120) + AV	7.5 (29%)	10.3 (0%)	17.8 (12%)	3.18	1984-95 B, AV	175	6.3
Finland	1998	FMK	WAVE	6.9 (24%)	8.4 (10%)	15.3 (16%)	2.76	1982-98 WAVE	234	3.8
France	1996	FF	WAVE	8.1 (20%)	7.8 (6%)	15.9 (15%)	3.11	1991-96 WAVE	55	7.0
Germany	1997	GDM	B (120)+ AV	2.93 (9%)	n.a.	n.a.	1.69	1992-97 PWS	36	3.8
Greece	1995	GDR	B (204)	188 (22%)	75 (22%)	263 (22%)	1.14	1990-95 AB	114	2.2
Hungary	1997	HFL	AV	73.3 (0%)	52.2 (0%)	125.5 (0%)	0.82	1986-96 AV	3 293	18.7
Italy	1996	LIT	AV-65%	783 (4%)	518 (0%)	1 301 (2%)	0.84	1992-98 PWS-AV	39	2.0
Japan	1995	YY	WAV	141 (49%)	106	247	2.10	1990-98 AB	2.5	0.3
Korea	1996	W	WAV	201	90	291 (0%)	0.34	1992-96 V	45	2.6
Luxembourg	1994	FLUX	WAVE	36.1	n.a.	n.a.	1.01	1990-94 WAVE	42	6.0
Netherlands	1998	DFL	B (120) + AV	2.9 (22%)	3.6 (100%)	6.5 (65%)	3.16	1990-98 PWS	73	4.6
Spain	1994	Ptas	B (200) + AV	97	49	146	1.07	n.a.		
Sweden	1998	SEK	AB (200) + AV	8.3 (32%)	12.4 (32%)	20.7 (32%)	2.60	1991-98 AB (200)	35	1.9
Switzerland	1996	FS	WAVE	1.6			1.29	n.a.		
Turkey	1998	TRL	B (160)	264 000	132 000 (50%)	396 000	1.51	1990-98 WAV	25 344	153.1
								1993-98 WAV	2 190	-4.1
								1995-98 WAV	332	-24.5

OECD 1999

Table 13. **Household Tariffs: Levels and Recent Trends** *(cont.)*

		Water service prices per m³ (fixed element as % of total, in brackets)					Recent % increase		
	Currency	Measure	PWS	S&ST	Total	US$		Measure	Nominal	Real p.a.
UK:										
Eng. and Wales 1998-9	£	AB (130)	0.86	1.01	1.87	3.11	1994-98	AB	22	2.0
Scotland 1997-8	£	AB (140)	0.51	0.36	0.88	1.44	1993-97	AB	28	3.4
US 1997	US$	B (345)	0.58	0.67	1.25	1.25	1992-98	B-PWS	34	2.4

n.a. Not available.

Notes:
- S&ST: Sewerage and sewage treatment.
- Practices in countries vary considerably in terms of the costs that are included in these tariffs. For example, charges occasionally reflect some of the costs of connecting a property to the public water supply or sewerage system. Also, rainwater collection, treatment and disposal costs are frequently, but not invariably, included in sewerage and sewage treatment charges.
- Water abstraction and discharge charges, as well as other water levies, are reflected in tariffs.
- The Japanese consumption tax (5%) is also included; but VAT is excluded.
- High inflation rates in some countries (e.g. Turkey, Hungary, and the Czech Republic) will reduce the precision of cross-country price comparisons.

Measures used:

AB(x) Average bill covering flat rate and metered households with an estimated average consumption of x m³/year.
AV   Unweighted average of volumetric rates.
AV-P   Weighted average of household bills covering P% of population.
A-B   Average household bill, converted to volumetric rate, with consumption changing over time.
B(y)   Average bill when household consumption is y m³/year.
WAV   Weighted average of volumetric rates.
WAVE   Weighted average of volumetric rates, and of volumetric charge equivalent to average fixed charge.
"COW" Cost of Water, as defined by sources in the Belgium submission to this study.

between zero (for **Belgium**, the **Czech Republic**, **Denmark**, **Hungary**, and **Italy**) and 100 per cent (for the **Netherlands** and, effectively, **Australia**). For combined bills, only three countries show a proportion of fixed charges above 25 per cent: **Sweden** (32 per cent), the **Netherlands** (65 per cent) and **Australia** (69 per cent). In each of these countries, however, there are moves currently underway to change this situation – moves which would increase the force of the conservation message. **Sweden**, for example, is already considering the introduction of a volumetric tax. Similarly, the possible development of a single volumetric charge for the **Netherlands** – the *Waterspoor* – was discussed above.

It is also useful to think of the situation in dynamic terms. The second part of Table 13 illustrates recent changes in households' average combined bills in a number of countries (for **Germany** and **Luxembourg**, only PWS data was available). Consumer Price Index data from the IMF and OECD has been used to convert nominal (money) increases into "real" changes, which have been expressed on an "annual equivalent" basis.

Denmark's average combined bills increased by 6.3 per cent per annum in real terms over the 1984-95 period. Denmark provides an interesting example of a country that has recently been obliged to start to address water quality problems by attempting to manage quantity (Box 11).

Table 13 also illustrates that **France** experienced very large real increases in water charges in the first half of the 1990s, largely due to the impending implementation (1998-2005) of the European Commission's Urban Waste Water Treatment Directive (Cambon-Grau and Berland, 1998). Indeed, over 1991-96, the PWS share of the average increase in the (nominal) water bill rose by 31 per cent, while the wastewater element increased by 90 per cent, according to a government survey covering a sample of 738 communes, and representing over 40 per cent of the French population (ministère de l'Économie et des Finances, 1996). Simultaneously, it seems, household water consumption was probably stabilising, or even falling slightly in the first half of the 1990s, after increasing through the 1980s.

In **Turkey**, while real per annum price increases of over 153 per cent have occurred over the period 1990-98, when this is disaggregated, it becomes clear that the real change has been much less in recent years, with an estimated annual *reduction* in prices between 1993 and 1998. *Per capita* household water consumption has, however, continued to increase, despite these changes in water prices.

Hungary's large real price increases (18.7 per cent per annum over the period 1986-1996) were caused mainly by increased restrictions on the application of subsidies to household water consumption after 1992 (Raskoli, 1998). Overall, as charges have increased in Hungary, consumption has fallen, from 154 lhd to 102 lhd, between 1986 and 1997 (Table 1).

81

Box 11.   Tariff Levels in Denmark

There is no shortage of water in **Denmark,** and virtually all of the public water supply is taken from groundwater sources. These resources, however, are of declining quality, and this has been posing serious problems for waterworks in certain regions for several years (*e.g.* the Island of Zealand).

In the 1980s, water charges in Denmark were perceived to be very low, such that in 1988 it was suggested that within Western Europe, only **Spain** and **Italy** had lower charges (IWSA, 1988). By 1995, however, Denmark had the highest overall "equivalent-volumetric" rate per cubic metre in all the OECD countries for which data were available. Moreover, in that calculation: *i*) the new water tax was still only charged at 2 DKr/m^3; *ii*) the sewage levy had not yet been introduced; and *iii*) no account was taken of the 25 per cent VAT charge which prevails in Denmark.

An estimate for 1998 should now include the three remaining "tranches" of the full water tax (now at 5 DKr/m^3), the sewage levy (introduced on 1 January 1997), and the 25 per cent VAT applied to all charges in the final bill. Even assuming that underlying water supply and wastewater costs have remained the same in nominal terms over 1995-98, a combined average volumetric rate of DKr 27.9/m^3 can be found in 1998. At May 1998 exchange rates, this is equivalent to US$4.13/m^3, or 30 per cent higher than any other rate found in Table 13.

In addition to these new tax and "volumetric rate" policies, domestic metering has become more widespread in Denmark, and information campaigns to promote water economy have been given prominence. The combined effect of these initiatives can be clearly observed in Table 1, where estimated household consumption is found to have decreased from 175 lhd to 139 lhd over the period 1987-96 – a reduction of 20 per cent.

If reliable inflation data had been available for the **Czech Republic,** a similar story of subsidy restriction (certainly true), sizeable increases in real charges (very probably true), and *per capita* consumption reductions (18 per cent between 1992-97; see Table 1), could probably have been told. Evidence is available to show that a similar, but less dramatic, pattern also emerged in **Luxembourg** over the period 1990-94. Here, PWS charges rose 6 per cent per annum in real terms, overall cost recovery rose from 75 per cent to 85 per cent, and reported household consumption fell from 181 lhd to 169 lhd between 1990 and 1995.

Industrial tariff levels

In order to compare industrial water prices across OECD countries, an index of industrial water prices (including several "typical" pricing circumstances) was developed. For each of the eight OECD countries[11] examined, key features were identified which might influence industrial water prices. An attempt was made to ensure that these factors reflected both the price range available in a given country (by taking information from the lowest and highest price locations), as well as information on population densities and relative levels of industrialisation (by taking information from the capital area, an industrial area, and a rural area). For each of these "domains", the bill faced by a typical industrial user was then calculated (including taxes and charges), divided according to three different types of user[12] – small, medium and large. The average price per unit of consumption for each type of user in each charging system was then calculated.

Because of data availability and accuracy problems, these indices have somewhat limited applicability. For example, the individual country indices do not incorporate any measure of the relative quality of service (*e.g.* reliability) offered in each country, so they cannot be used to draw any conclusions about the relative "value-for-money" offered by water suppliers in the different countries.

Furthermore, the fact that direct abstractions account for the greater proportion of water use by industry also means that these indexes (being based as they are on industry's limited use of the *public* water supply) could be misleading, especially if applied to specific locations. For this reason, no results are provided here concerning actual price levels within individual countries. On the other hand, it is interesting to review the way in which industrial water prices seem to vary according to type of user and/or location (Table 14).

Table 14. **Industrial Water Price Level Variations**
By User Type and By Location For 8 OECD Countries

(USD/m³)	Small user	Medium user	Large user
The capital city	0.92	0.95	0.83
An industrial area	1.00	0.99	0.87
A rural area	0.85	0.83	0.78
National average	0.88	0.97	0.81
Minimum	0.55	0.45	0.40
Maximum	1.51	1.72	1.59

From this analysis, it appears that large industrial users in the countries examined tend to obtain slightly lower prices (on average) than smaller users. In general, prices in industrial areas are also higher than those in rural areas for all categories of users.

Agricultural tariff levels

Comparing agricultural price levels across countries and regions is a difficult exercise, unless these comparisons are put into an appropriate context. Ultimately, the price of agricultural water should depend on how productive water is to irrigators. This productivity will depend on a number of attributes associated with the water supply, including:

- water quality;
- level of uncertainty in fulfilling contracted allotments;
- frequency and certainty of water availability for field applications;
- technological conditions of any metering devices;
- discrepancies between charged volumes and accessible volumes at farm-gates; and
- water pressure.

Thus, when comparing agricultural water price levels, it would be desirable to acompany per-volume or per-surface price level data with a description of some of these attributes.[13]

Table 15 summarises some price data on irrigation water pertaining to several OECD countries. Among the countries included in this table, **Canada** and **New Zealand** and **Australia** have the lowest prices, although the reasons for this vary. Except in Alberta (comprising about 70 per cent of **Canada's** total irrigated land), water resources are abundant enough in Canada that irrigation districts can easily tap into nearby water bodies to supply their farmers. Because water is so abundant, there is little competition for water, and supply costs are therefore typically very low. As a result, Canadian irrigation prices are also low, and are usually based on flat-rates. Furthermore, there is not much need to meter farmers' consumption, and the use of marginal cost pricing would probably be quite inefficient, considering the application costs likely to be associated with such an approach.

In **New Zealand,** water resources are also abundant, but here, the irrigation companies have been fully privatised. The result is somewhat higher prices than those which exist in **Canada.** These retail companies, some of which are owned by the irrigators themselves, are required to charge "full cost recovery" prices. However, those companies whose assets were created before privatisation took place only need to charge capital replacement costs on top of O&M costs. This is because the handing over of irrigation assets to farmers and users' associations was not intended to maximise the government's returns, but to ensure that the privatised districts would remain operational. The net result, therefore, is that the capital costs recovered in this case include only those associated with investments made after the irrigation district was handed over to its final private owners.

Australia's water pricing policy is unique among the semi-arid OECD countries, in that it requires full cost recovery. Curiously, the water charges that result in Australia from the application of the full cost recovery principle turn out to be much lower than in countries which do not yet apply this criterion. This seeming

Table 15. **Agricultural Water Price Ranges and Characteristics in Selected OECD Countries**

	Region (year)	Supply characteristics	Type of charge	Price (in $) Surf. (per ha)	Price (in $) Vol. (m³)	Cost-recovery	Comments	Sources
Australia	N.S.Wales (95)	Wholesale + min. charge	Volume (low security)	–	0.0024	100% O&M + CD	Includes resource management	Musgrave (1997)
	N.S.Wales (95)	Wholesale + min. charge	Volume (high security)	–	0.0028	100% O&M + CD	Includes resource management	Musgrave (1997)
	Queensland (95)	Wholesale	Volume	–	0.00739	100% O&M		Musgrave (1997)
	Murray-Darling (92)	Wholesale	Volume	–	0.010	60% O&M	Since 1992, prices rose by 11%	Musgrave (1997)
	National average (96)	n.a.	Two-part	0.75-2.27	0.0195	Variable	Most representative figure	Dinar and Subramanian (1997)
Austria	National average (98)	Retail (from municipalities – waterpipes)	Volume	–	0.23-1.78	100% O&M	Livestock consumption	Rech (1998); Breindl (1998)
Canada	Saskachewan (98)	Retail	Surface	10.5-14.9	–	100% O&M	In federally owned districts	PFRA (1998)
	British Columbia (88)	Wholesale	Surface	90	–	< 100% O&M	In publicly developed districts	Horbulyk (1998)
	British Columbia (88)	Wholesale	Volume	–	0.00016-0.0002	< 100% O&M	In publicly developed districts	Horbulyk (1998)
	Alberta (98)	Retail	Surface	12.2-26.7	–	100% O&M	In farmer-controlled districts	PFRA (1998)
	National average (96)	n.a.	Two-part	6.62-36.65	0.0017-0.002	100% O&M	Most representative figure	Dinar and Subramanian (1997)
France	Adour-Garon W.A (97)	Wholesale (replenished watercourse)	Volume	–	0.00527	100% O&M	Water abstracted for irrigation	Duchein (1997)
	Adour-Garon W.A (97)	Wholesale (groundwater)	Fixed	–	0.0046	100% O&M	Water abstracted for irrigation	Duchein (1997)
	C.d.Côteaux de Gascogne (93)	Wholesale	Fixed (equiv. prices)	–	0.158	100% O&M	Water abstracted for irrigation	Montginoul and Rieu (1996)
	Rhôn-Med.Cor.W.A. (94)	Wholesale (surface)	Fixed (equiv. prices)	–	0.0031	100% O&M	In Provence, to irrigate 50 ha	Montginoul (1997)
	Rhôn-Med.Cor.W.A. (94)	Wholesale (ground)	Fixed (equiv. prices)	–	0.0065	100% O&M	In Provence, to irrigate 50 ha	Montginoul (1997)
	Canal de Provence (93)	Wholesale	Fixed (equiv. prices)	–	0.11	100% O&M + cap	Varies, depending on factors	Montginoul (1997)
Greece	Crete (OADYK) (97)	Retail	Surface	–	0.021	100% O&M	Self-financed public company	Lekakis (1998)
	Crete (OADYK) (97)	Retail (pumping)	Surface	–	0.082	100% O&M	Self-financed public company	Lekakis (1998)
	National aver. (97)	Retail	Surface	92-210	–	60-75% O&M	In publicly developed districts	Seliantis (1997)

Table 15. **Agricultural Water Price Ranges and Characteristics in Selected OECD Countries** *(cont.)*

	Region (year)	Supply characteristics	Type of charge	Price (in $) Surf. (per ha)	Price (in $) Vol. (m³)	Cost-recovery	Comments	Sources
Italy	Northwest (94)	Retail	Surface	32.67	–	93% O&M	Average Consortia Data	Destro (1997)
	Northwest (94)	Retail	Surface	53.11	–	64% O&M	Average Consortia Data	Destro (1997)
	Nurra-Serdegna (94)	Retail	Two-part (citrus)	250	–	n.a.	Consortia Data	Aiello et al. (1995)
	Nurra-Serdegna (94)	Retail	Two-part (drip sys)	62.4	–	n.a.	Consortia Data	Aiello et al. (1995)
	Nurra-Serdegna (94)	Retail	Two-part (melon)	125	–	n.a.	Consortia Data	Aiello et al. (1995)
Japan	National average (97)	Retail	Surface (rice grwr's)	246	–	100% O&M + part of cap	Most representative figure	Nakashima (1997)
Mexico	National average (97)	Retail	Surface	60	–	68-80% O&M	Most representative figure	Johnson (1997)
	Cortazar (97)	Retail	Surface	33	–	73% O&M	Transferred irrigation module	Johnson (1997)
Netherlands	National average (98)	Wholesale + Retail	Surface and Groundwater		1.44	> 100% O&M	Most representative figure	National Reference Centre for Agriculture (1998)
New Zealand	Lower Waitaki	Retail	Surface	11-27.5	–	100% O&M + cap	Irrigation companies	Scrimgeour (1997)
Portugal	Sorria (97)	Wholesale	One-or two- part (rice)	173-208(a)	0.010	100% O&M	In publicly developed districts	Bragança (1998)
	Sorria (97)	Wholesale	Two-part (maize)	105(b)	0.014(c)	100% O&M	In publicly developed districts	Bragança (1998)
	Sorria (97)	Wholesale	Two-part (tomatoes)	136(b)	0.025(c)	100% O&M	In publicly developed districts	Bragança (1998)
	Vigia (97)	Wholesale	One-part (maize) (sprinkler irrigation)	–	0.042(d)	< 100% O&M	In publicly developed districts	Bragança (1998)
Spain	Andalucia Gen-Cab (95)	Wholesale + Retail (pump)	2-part (sprinklers)	90	0.027-	100% O&M	A modern public district	Sumpsi et al. (1996)
	Andalucia. Viar (95)	Wholesale + Retail	Surface	113	–	100% O&M	An old private district	Sumpsi et al. (1996)
	Valencia Ac.Real (95)	Wholesale + Retail	Surface	142.92	–	100% O&M	Historical irrigation district	Sumpsi et al. (1996)
	Valencia Novelda (95)	Retail (groundwater)	Two-part	90	0.133	100% O&M + cap	Privately built for speciality crops	Sumpsi et al. (1996)
	Castille. Retencion (95)	Wholesale + Retail	Surface	90	–	100% O&M	A publicly developed district	Sumpsi et al. (1996)
	Castille. Villalar (95)	Retail (groundwater)	Vol. (+ energy)		0.07	100% O&M	A publicly developed district	Sumpsi et al. (1996)

Table 15. **Agricultural Water Price Ranges and Characteristics in Selected OECD Countries** *(cont.)*

Region (year)	Supply characteristics	Type of charge	Price (in $) Surf. (per ha)	Price (in $) Vol. (m³)	Cost-recovery	Comments	Sources
Turkey							
Mediterranean (98)	Wholesale + Retail	(Cotton) surface	49.50	–	70% O&M	WUA transferred from DSI	DSI and WUAs (1998)
Mediterranean (98)	Wholesale + Retail	(Cotton) pumping	96.50	–	70% O&M	WUA transferred from DSI	DSI and WUAs (1998)
Central Anatolia (98)	Wholesale + Retail	(Wheat) surface	19.80	–	70% O&M	WUA transferred from DSI	DSI and WUAs (1998)
South-East Anatolia (98)	Wholesale + Retail	(Wheat) pumping	44.00	–	70% O&M	WUA transferred from DSI	DSI and WUAs (1998)
UK							
Northumbria (97)	Abstraction charges	Volumetric	–	0.028	100% Costs	Minimum annual charge $42 +	Environmental Agency (1997)
Northumbria (97)	Abstraction charges	Vol. (+ equip used in summer)	–	0.136	100% Costs	Application charge $167	
Wales (97)	Abstraction charges	Volumetric	–	0.013	100% Costs		
US							
N. Sacramento River (CA) (97)	Wholesale + min. charge	Vol. up to 80%	–	0.0049 + 0.011	100% O&M	Central Valley Improvement Act	Wahl (1997)
N. Sacramento River (CA) (97)	Wholesale + min. charge	Vol. up to 80-90%	–	0.0049 + 0.014	100% O&M	Central Valley Improvement Act	Wahl (1997)
N. Sacramento River (CA) (97)	Wholesale + min. charge	Vol. up to 90-100%	–	0.0049 + 0.016	100% O&M + cap	Central Valley Improvement Act	Wahl (1997)
Tehama.Col. CI (CA) (97)	Wholesale + min. charge	Vol. up to 80%	–	0.0049 + 0.025	100% O&M	Central Valley Improvement Act	Wahl (1997)
Tehama.Col. CI (CA) (97)	Wholesale + min. charge	Vol. up to 80-90%	–	0.0049 + 0.048	100% O&M	Central Valley Improvement Act	Wahl (1997)
Tehama.Col. CI (CA) (97)	Wholesale + min. charge	Vol. up to 90-100%	–	0.0049 + 0.071	100% O&M + cap	Central Valley Improvement Act	Wahl (1997)
Pacific North West (90)	Wholesale	Average	13.4	–	17% of total costs	B of R average for 1.1 mill ha.	Schaible (1997)

Notes:
– All currencies have been converted to US dollars, using exchange rates shown in *The Economist* (first issue of March 1998), unless the source provides the figure directly in dollar terms, in which case the figure has been transposed to this Table as it appears in the source.
– Some figures which appear as Vol. (m³) might have originated from surface pricing, but were then converted into volumetric ones, using the estimated consumed volumes.
– Portugal: *a)* the maximum value was derived by adding the drainage tax (US$35/ha) wherever it is applied to the consumption estimated volumetric cost (for 17 200 m³ at US$0.01/m³; *b)* these values were derived by adding the extra crop taxes (maize: US$33/ha, tomatoes: US$82/ha) to the volumetric costs; *c)* these values were derived based on the estimated water volumes, the value per m³ and the extra crop taxes for maize and tomatoes; and *d)* in this project, the tax is paid in accordance with water volumes and the value of m³ is fixed yearly for the majority of irrigated crops.

contradiction can be explained by two factors. One is that the "grandfathering" provisions included in the Australian reforms were quite generous to already-established irrigators, so that the definition of full cost recovery for irrigation systems is rather narrow, especially regarding capital costs. The other factor might be that water supply costs are themselves lower than in other semi-arid countries, such as **Spain** or the **US**.

Of course, the fact that water prices turn out to be only moderately high does not negate the importance of the Australian example. An interesting feature of how water rights have been defined in some Australian States is that irrigators can hold low- as well as high-security water rights. This is useful, because it allows irrigators to adapt their individual farm situations to their cropping patterns, without introducing excessive complexity into the market-based system itself. The price spread among both types of rights is only US cents 0.04 per m^3, indicating that (in New South Wales at least) both sets of rights enjoy very similar levels of supply guarantee.

Portuguese pricing policies are severely constrained by the fact that most of that country's irrigated acreage has been privately developed. In publicly-developed irrigation districts, water prices have therefore been tailored to specific crops and irrigated techniques, conforming with the "ability-to-pay" principle, but still managing to raise some revenues with which to ease the government's financial burden. The water pricing criteria which will ultimately be applied in the new Alqueva project are still undefined. Since the **European Union** is financing a part of these costs, it will be interesting to see how the EU Framework Water Directive's principles are eventually applied to the beneficiaries of that project. Overall, irrigation policy in Portugal is driven mostly by agricultural and rural development policies, rather than by natural resource management objectives.

In **Turkey,** water rates discriminate among irrigated crops and irrigation techniques. While prices are set (in principle) to recover 100 per cent of O&M costs, in practice, a rate of only 70 per cent is realised. As mentioned above, a considerable portion of publicly developed irrigation lands have now been transferred to Water User Associations, who set prices to include expected future (rather than past) O&M costs, as well as some investment costs. As a result, cost recovery is improving significantly under the new arrangements. Turkey is now at the stage of water development that the **US, Spain,** and **Australia** underwent 30-40 years ago. Generating market returns, or even just avoiding capital losses, on irrigation projects is now becoming as important as either settling farmers on less-favourable lands, or improving the country's position as a major agricultural exporter.

Overall, **Greece** takes a similar approach to that of Portugal and Turkey, in that it actively encourages agricultural and rural development with its water pricing strategies. However, the Greek case is somewhat more complex, mainly because its

OECD 1999

hydrologic characteristics are much more challenging. Also, while water charges are much higher in Greece than in Portugal or Turkey, Greek farmers operating in publicly developed irrigation units still do not fully cover O&M or capital replacement costs.

Irrigation water prices in **Japan** are well above those existing in most other OECD countries. Access to irrigation water is vital for paddy growers, who generally operate in a highly structured landholding system. Although water rates are typically flat, water is scrupulously distributed among district farmers, and under fairly stressful natural conditions. Also, since marginal application costs are high, farmers generally refrain from using excessive volumes of water. The deterioration of many old irrigation districts' collective assets is a result of the inability to raise enough revenues to match (generally increasing) maintenance costs. Nakashima (1997) singles out co-ordination failures among a large number of dispersed farmers as the major explanatory factor behind inadequate capital replacement and maintenance activities. The option of allowing water transfers to urban suppliers, in return for capital investments in the districts' infrastructures, is also being exploited in some situations.

In the **Netherlands,** average water supply charges for agricultural water users amount to US$1.44 per m^3, with farmers required to pay the full supply costs and, where appropriate, the full drainage costs as well.

In **England and Wales,** farmers are on an equal footing with other water users, although only those farmers who install acceptable metering devices and procedures are charged rates in accordance with actual consumed volumes. (The metering of water in the UK is still rare for the agricultural sector.) Charges are set by the water companies, which make each user responsible for its own costs. Cost recovery does take place in most areas, although in the Thames region water charges are estimated to be well below long-run marginal costs (Rees, 1997). However, imposing incentive charges greater than current costs is not legally permitted at the moment. Hence, if the EU Framework Water Directive is passed in its current form (see earlier discussion), and then transposed into UK Law, these price ceilings may need to be removed.

Italy exhibits two basic approaches to water pricing policy. In the (northern) Po Valley, water prices do not even cover O&M costs. Here, the development of irrigated land was the result of a long-standing public objective to reclaim large marsh areas prone to disease, with the government covering all capital costs for irrigation projects. In the drier (southern) areas, of which the Capitanata region is a representative example, water is distributed on the basis of fairly strict quotas, even to the point of being taken away from those irrigators who consistently exceed their targets. At the national level, a recently-passed Framework Law on Waters seems to provide a means for implementing pricing policies that bring the collected

89

revenues nearer to O&M and investment costs (although this only applies to pub licly supplied water, while irrigation water is primarily supplied through Water Use Associations). In principle, this Law does not seem substantially different from the proposed EU Framework Water Directive.

In **Mexico,** although water charges paid by farmers are currently increasing, they are still relatively low by OECD standards. During the thirty years prior to the 1990s prices lagged behind inflation rates, and the coverage of actual irrigation costs was very low. With the ambitious devolution program of irrigation district management to the recently created "irrigation modules", charges will probably increase. One problem encountered with volumetric charging in Mexico is that when drought conditions force the downward revision of the water volumes to which water right holders are entitled, the amount of revenue collected also declines. Hence, regions which are vulnerable to natural water shortages will also experience difficulties in matching "modules" costs for some time to come. On balance, irrigation water prices in Mexico will probably be limited to levels which cover total O&M costs, at least over the medium-term.

Irrigation pricing policies in **France** vary considerably between areas. Water companies have quite a long experience of supplying water services to irrigators and of charging differential prices based on the costs companies incur in servicing their customers. Inasmuch as French basins are quite heterogeneous, it is not sur- prising that water companies would use completely differing pricing criteria, and therefore end up charging quite different price levels. Some companies operating in basins with large natural supply variations tend to combine prices with quotas, with the size of the quota depending on each season's water availability for irrigation.

The 1992 Water Law in France empowers companies and River Basin Agencies to levy environmental taxes as well as volume-based charges. This Law aims to make all water users, whether consumptive or non-consumptive, responsible for the full costs they impose on water systems. A slight inconsistency results from the fact that, despite significant recent efforts to raise water use charges, irrigation farming is still increasing, in part because of programmes which offer subsidies to farmers who invest in new irrigation equipment.

Spain is perhaps the most heterogeneous example among the countries surveyed in this report. The prices reported in Table 15 for Spain include wholesale charges collected by the public basin agencies, as well as the retail prices that farm- ers pay to their irrigation districts. Typically, price variations across basins and irri- gation districts are explained by the relative accessibility to the water source by different irrigation technologies, and by how old the irrigation district is. But even taking these factors into account, retail prices vary significantly across districts, some of which are located very near to each other.

Even in regions with relatively plentiful water resources (*e.g.* Castille), prices are in the upper range of those indicated in Table 15. At the other extreme, farmers in the arid south-east are using desalinised water at US$0.6-0.8 per m³ to irrigate speciality crops grown under completely artificial and closed-system conditions. Preliminary evaluations indicate that the application of the EU Framework Water Directive would eliminate entire irrigation areas, leaving others almost indifferent, simply because net returns are well in excess of US$20-30 000 per hectare, and water prices already cover their total supply costs.

Agricultural water prices in the **US** are as variable, complex, and diverse as they are in Spain. Those farmers who hold historical rights pay little more than the specific costs incurred in retailing water within the irrigation districts. Apart from California and a few other States which exploit groundwater resources (among which the most important is Texas), public pricing policies are virtually non-existent in the US. Other than in these cases, irrigators located in publicly developed water districts of the Western States pay reduced prices, but which are sufficient to cover at least the districts' O&M costs.

California's water economy situation finds no similar examples elsewhere in the world – it encompasses extreme situations which range from farmers irrigating alfalfa in the dry Imperial Valley near the border with Mexico, to electronically supported water marketing systems in the San Joaquin Valley (Olmstead *et al.*, 1997). The California Water Agency has offered the world one of the most commented-upon water banking experiments. This simple price-incentive scheme was sufficient to encourage the exchange of more than 700 million cubic metres of water in just a few months. However, public pricing policies began to be used only after the passage of the Central Valley Improvement Act of 1992. As a result of this Act, tiered-pricing was introduced with some success in several publicly developed irrigation districts (Wilchens, 1991). However, the implemented price levels are fairly moderate in view of the other prices reported in Table 15. In sum, despite a few significant experiences, irrigation water pricing has not been given the importance in the US that already exists in Australia, or that might exist in the EU, if the Framework Water Directive is eventually implemented.

OECD 1999

Chapter 6

Direct Abstractions

6.1. Sources of industrial water

In principle, industrial water users can choose either to take water at the price being offered by public suppliers, or to invest in water abstraction and treatment facilities, and to supply their own water. Direct abstractions appear to be more advantageous than public supplies for the majority of OECD industrial users (Figure 4).

Korea and **Luxembourg** are the only countries where direct abstractions do not dominate in the industrial sector. In Luxembourg, the recent decline in heavy industry activity might account for the stronger reliance on public supplies (probably driven by the small business community).

Several reasons underlie the preference for direct abstractions by industrial users. First, the quality of water required by industrial users might differ substantially from that which must be achieved in the public supply network, where water must be of potable quality. Piped water is produced at very high drinking water quality standards, and these standards have been gradually tightened over recent years. This supply does not fit the needs of many industrial concerns, which can often use water of lower quality – it is only in the food and beverage industry that water used must generally be of drinking water quality.

There are only a few examples of countries where piped water of varying quality standards is supplied. In **Korea,** for instance, the price of publicly supplied water varies according to the type of treatment applied to the water that is provided (raw, filtered, or purified). This reflects the fact that, public supply is designed to be diverse enough to meet different demands. In the **Netherlands,** in addition to drinking water, water of other degrees of quality is also distributed on a limited scale by water companies, such as non- and semi-filtered water, and distilled and demineralised surface water. In 1995, seven water supply companies distributed 62.3 million m^3 of this "other water", mostly to industrial users which do not require drinking water quality standard inputs.

OECD 1999

Figure 4. Public Supply vs. Direct Abstractions for Industrial Water in Selected OECD Countries

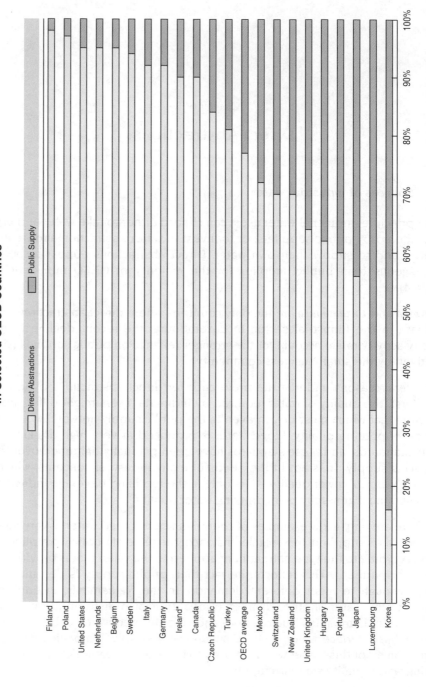

Note: * Data on industrial water use was not broken down between publicly supplied water and directly abstracted water for *Ireland*, so the percentage of wastewater discharged directly was used as a proxy indicator for the percentage of water abstracted directly.

Second, particularly for non-consumptive uses, it is often easier for industries to abstract water directly from surface waters near the plant, and to discharge it back to the point of supply with minimum treatment. The cost of doing this tends to be cheaper than using publicly supplied water.

Third, the dominance of direct abstractions is probably influenced by the fact that, whereas public water prices may sometimes discriminate against industrial users (and have recently been increased to reflect higher quality requirements), abstraction charges for industrial users are usually administratively-based instead of reflecting the economic costs of water used by industry. As a result, over a certain threshold, it is cheaper for industrial users to invest in water abstraction and treatment facilities than to pay for publicly supplied water.

One important consequence of the dominance of direct abstractions is that water prices for a large percentage of industrial water users can be difficult to ascertain, because the costs of direct abstractions vary widely from one industrial concern to another, and data about these costs are not easily accessible (the information is often not public). In most cases, direct abstraction and discharge charges are the only proxies which can be used to compare costs for self-supplied water between OECD countries.

The physical source of industrial water abstractions can be either groundwater or surface water. Figure 5 shows that on average (across those OECD countries for which sufficient data was available), 62 per cent of industrial water abstractions come from surface water, and 38 per cent from groundwater. The choice made by industrial users about which source to use depends on two main factors: the investment and operating costs of directly abstracting water (setting up of abstraction facilities, boreholes, or pipes) and the abstraction charge levied by environmental regulators (which usually varies according to the source of abstraction).

Industrial users will tend to access the cheapest resource first (*i.e.* the source for which investment and operating costs are minimised). The relative costs of the two alternatives also depend on the specific resource situation existing in each country. Although surface water is commonly used, it is not always cheaper. In **Denmark,** for instance, 99 per cent of freshwater resources are abstracted from groundwater because groundwater resources are extremely abundant, although conservation measures have recently tried to limit this use due to the growing pollution of aquifers.

The source chosen by industry also depends on the relative costs of direct abstractions for industrial users through variations in abstraction charges (where these apply). Depending on the relative scarcity of groundwater versus surface water, environmental regulators may set different levels of abstraction charges. In several Länder in **Germany,** for instance, groundwater abstraction charges are higher than surface water abstraction charges. This may or may not be related to a net shift in industrial abstractions from groundwater sources to surface water ones.

95

Figure 5. **Physical Sources of Industrial Water in Selected OECD Countries**

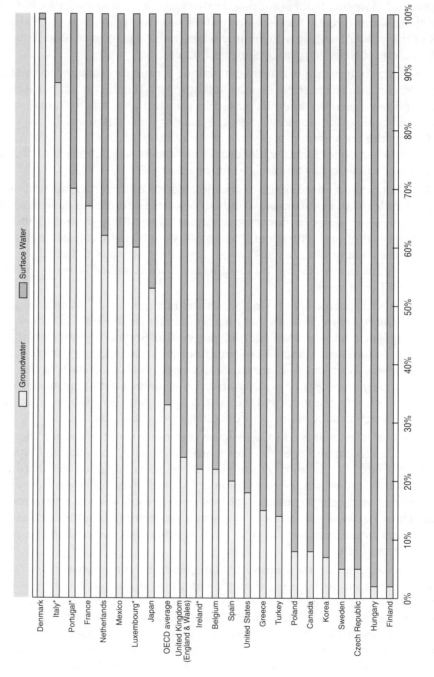

Note: * Data for the physical source was derived from the data applying to all water uses. For *Italy*, the data is also limited to water sourced from the public supply system.

In the **UK**, on the other hand, surface water abstraction charges from some sources[14] are weighted by a coefficient of 3, whereas groundwater abstractions are weighted by a coefficient of only 1, with the result that the abstraction charge is higher for surface water. It is not clear that the behaviour of industrial users has been significantly influenced by these differential charges, since 76 per cent of water directly abstracted by UK industry still comes from surface water. In addition, the charges for both types of abstraction are quite low.

6.2.   Abstraction charges

Most OECD countries levy some form of charge and/or place restrictions on the direct abstraction of water use, although practices vary across countries and across sectors. Most explicitly differentiate between user types (industrial, agricultural or utilities for the provision of piped household water services), and apply different levels of abstraction charges accordingly. Charges can take the form of a nominal license fee linked to an abstraction permit regime, or they can be varied according to quantity criteria.

Agricultural water users often directly abstract the water they use for irrigation purposes themselves, or subscribe to a water users association which abstract and distribute the water for them. The rights farmers have to use water resources often vary across regions (depending on water availability) and between water sources (see Table 11 above). For example, water rights in some countries (*e.g.* **Spain**) are strongly connected to land use rights, while in other countries (*e.g.* **Canada** and **Australia**), it is possible to trade water use quotas between agricultural users. In a number of countries, farmers have free use of groundwater resources accessed through their properties (*e.g.* **Canada**), while in others, abstraction licenses are required (*e.g.* **Australia, Greece, Spain, Turkey,** and the **UK**). Most of the charges for direct abstractions of irrigation water are based on the issuance or renewal of abstraction licenses or water use quotas.

Eleven OECD countries [**Mexico, Japan, Belgium, France, Germany, Hungary, Italy,** the **Netherlands, Poland, Spain,** and the **UK** (**England and Wales**)] also levy an abstraction charge on piped *household* water services, and a similar charge is under discussion or planned in at least two others (**Portugal** and **Sweden**). These typically vary by category of use and often by location (they therefore sometimes reflect water scarcities). Since these charges often have a mainly environmental purpose, the proceeds are sometimes turned over to environmental agencies or environmental funds. The direct economic costs associated with abstraction support works may be recovered through standard abstraction charges (*e.g.* **England and Wales**), or they may have an explicitly environmental purpose (*e.g.* **Netherlands**). In the latter case, therefore, by enhancing these charges, costs for the water supplier can be reduced (as a result of demand responses to the environment-related charge), and cost-recovery increased.

97

Abstraction charges for *industrial* water use are in place in about half of OECD countries, including **Australia, Belgium, Canada,** the **Czech Republic, France, Germany, Hungary, Italy, Japan, Korea, Mexico,** the **Netherlands, Poland, Spain, Turkey,** and the **UK.** According to previous OECD studies (OECD, 1987a), they also

Table 16. **Charges for Industrial Water Abstraction**

	In place?	Where do funds go?	CAP	ACT	USE	Variations	TR
Australia	Yes	n.a.	Yes	Yes	n.a.	n.a.	Yes
Austria	Yes	d.n.a.	d.n.a.	d.n.a.	d.n.a.	d.n.a.	No
Belgium	Yes	Environment	No	Yes	No	No	No
Canada	Yes	Administrative costs	Yes	No	n.a.	n.a.	No
Czech Republic	Yes	Environment	n.a.	n.a.	Yes	Source, location	No
Denmark	n.a.	n.a.	n.a.	n.a.	n.a.	n.a.	No
Finland	No	d.n.a.	d.n.a.	d.n.a.	d.n.a.	d.n.a.	No
France	Yes	River Basin Agencies Environment	Yes	Yes	Yes	Source, location	No
Germany	Yes	Administrative costs	n.a.	n.a.	Yes	Source, location	No
Greece	No	d.n.a.	d.n.a.	d.n.a.	d.n.a.	d.n.a.	No
Hungary	Yes	Water Fund, Environment	No	Yes	Yes	n.a.	No
Iceland	n.a.	n.a.	n.a.	n.a.	n.a.	n.a.	No
Ireland	No	d.n.a.	d.n.a.	d.n.a.	d.n.a.	d.n.a.	No
Italy	Yes	Basin authorities	Yes	No	Yes	Rebate if water-saving technologies used	Yes
Japan	Yes	n.a.	n.a.	n.a.	n.a.	n.a.	No
Korea	Yes	Environment, Administrative costs	No	Yes	Yes	Source	No
Luxembourg	n.a.	n.a.	n.a.	n.a.	n.a.	n.a.	No
Mexico	Yes	n.a.	No	Yes	Yes	Location	No
Netherlands	Yes	Environment (Provinces) General taxation (State)	No	Yes	Yes	Rebate if prior infiltration	No
New Zealand	No	d.n.a.	d.n.a.	d.n.a.	d.n.a.	d.n.a.	Yes
Norway	n.a.	n.a.	n.a.	n.a.	n.a.	Permit conditions	No
Poland	Yes	Environment	n.a.	n.a.	Yes	Source, location	No
Portugal	No	d.n.a.	d.n.a.	d.n.a.	d.n.a.	d.n.a.	No
Spain	Yes	River basin agencies Administrative costs and environment	Yes	No	Yes	Water rights hierarchy, location	Yes
Sweden	No	d.n.a.	d.n.a.	d.n.a.	d.n.a.	d.n.a.	No
Switzerland	n.a.	n.a.	n.a.	n.a.	n.a.	n.a.	No
Turkey	Yes	General budget (state/municipal)	Yes	Yes	Yes	Water rights hierarchy, ownership	No
United Kingdom	Yes	Environment Administrative costs	Yes	No	Yes	Source, loss factor, seasonal	No
United States	n.a.	n.a.	n.a.	n.a.	n.a.	n.a.	Yes

n.a. Data not available.　　d.n.a. Does not apply.
Notes:
In place?:　Is there an abstraction charge for industrial water uses?
CAP:　　　Is the charge based on the capacity granted to the industrial user?
ACT:　　　Is the charge based on the actual use of water by the industrial user?
USE:　　　Do abstraction charge regimes differentiate between types of uses?
Variations:　Are there other variations in the abstraction charging regime?
TR:　　　　Is it possible to trade abstraction licences in some places?

exist in the **US,** but no new data to confirm this was provided for this particular study. Abstraction charges do not exist in countries where water is deemed to be relatively abundant (*e.g.* **Sweden, Finland,** and **New Zealand**). Many of the charges which do exist have only recently been introduced [**Germany** (1985), the **Netherlands** (1995), and **Mexico** (1997)]. **Portugal** has approved an abstraction charge, but has not yet implemented it.

Other abstraction charges are much older, such as in **France,** where River Basin Agencies were created in 1964, and where a particularly sophisticated regime of abstraction and consumption charges was set up, based on very precise zoning defined at the river basin level. In **Belgium,** abstraction charges vary depending on whether the water abstracted is for drinking water production or other uses, as well as according to the volumes of water used.

In **Canada,** small licence fees apply. Fees are paid to the Provinces for access to provincially owned waters, but they are typically sufficient only to recover the administrative costs of the system. In **Australia,** bulk water suppliers charge industrial users for abstracting water from rivers and groundwater. The charges are based both on the entitlement to abstract water and the amount used, where this is metered.

In other countries, charges have an explicit environmental objective, and the proceeds are allocated to an environmental fund, as in **Belgium,** the **Czech Republic, France, Hungary,** and the **Netherlands.** In the **Netherlands,** there are two abstraction charges: one is levied by the Provinces, with the revenues being used for research related to groundwater depletion; the other is levied by the state, within the general taxation regime. In **Belgium,** the proceeds from abstraction charges in the regions of both Flanders and Wallonia are given to environmental funds which finance wastewater collection and wastewater treatment plants in Flanders, and the protection of groundwater resources in Wallonia.

Abstraction charge regimes can apply either to "capacity" (based on the allowed capacity allocated through a permit) or to "actual use", which requires metering and monitoring. In **France,** there are two distinct charges: an abstraction charge, based on volumes declared by users in advance; and a use charge, which varies according to the actual level of consumption. Where charges are paid in relation to permit systems, they tend to be set on the basis of maximum allowable intakes.

Abstraction charges can also vary according to the type of use. Industrial uses are not necessarily specifically differentiated: in the **Czech Republic,** the distinction is between consumptive and non-consumptive uses (but not according to user category). In **France,** consumption coefficients are calculated (for public supply, industry, power generation, agriculture), and then used in the calculation of the abstraction charges.

When distinctions by type of user *are* made, industrial uses tend to face higher charges than domestic ones (in **Poland**, for instance, abstraction charges for public supply are 6-47 times lower than those for industrial supply). On the other hand, water-intensive industries in **Germany** can obtain rebates. In the **Netherlands**, if surface water is injected into the aquifer before groundwater abstraction, the abstractor can claim a subsidy, which will then reduce the total charge. Similarly, in **Italy**, industrial users are all charged the same, but a 50 per cent reduction is given if water-saving techniques are employed.

Regional variations have been introduced in order to better manage resources on the basis of relative scarcity. These regional variations exist in most countries which have adopted an abstraction regime, and they contribute to the extremely diverse water price structures faced by industrial users. Seasonal variations are more rare (they exist in the **UK**), but they play a similar role where they do exist.

Finally, abstraction charge regimes can vary according to the source of supply (*i.e.* whether water comes from groundwater or surface water). Thus, charges are levied only on groundwater abstractors in the Wallonia Region of **Belgium**. Charges may also be levied for each source by different bodies: in the **Czech Republic**, Water Basin Companies levy the surface water abstraction charge, and the State Fund of Environment levies the groundwater abstraction charge (higher charges apply to groundwater).

Some countries allow the trading of abstraction permits, in order to better organise water resource management. These experiences are still relatively localised (California in the **US**; irrigated areas in **Spain**; some States in **Australia**), and there is no fully developed nation-wide scheme in any OECD country.

Chapter 7

Sewerage and Sewage Disposal

7.1. Domestic sewerage and sewage treatment

Selected information on tariff structures for household sewerage and sewage treatment systems in OECD countries is presented in Table 17. The pricing schemes in use are not always clear, largely because sewerage and sewage treatment are sometimes the responsibility of different agencies, each with their own charging schemes (see Box 12 for an example of the problems this complexity can generate).

However, available evidence indicates that, for 22 OECD countries, revenues for these services are based largely on volumetric charges, although they are generally directly related to volumes of water *supplied* by the public water system, rather than wastewater levels. Because the input of water to domestic residences has been found to be a close proxy for the volume of sewage generated, sewerage and sewage disposal charges are generally calculated as a function of the water supplied to households. Thus, the structure of wastewater charging regimes tends to follow closely that of domestic water supply systems in most OECD countries.

A greater proportion of wastewater revenues are now being recovered through volumetric charging, reflecting the continuing trend toward more incentive-based charging for the public water supply, and reinforcing incentives to use water supplies more carefully. This pressure is being further enhanced in certain OECD countries by other factors. Thus, purely volumetric levies for domestic wastewater services at the regional level in **Belgium** will soon have completely replaced other more complex (and less direct) mechanisms.

Similarly, a decision was taken in **Italy** in 1996 to levy sewerage and sewage treatment charges on 100 per cent of invoiced water, rather than on only 80 per cent. Indeed, if the 1994 water law proposed in Italy for the reorganisation of the public water system is passed, the increasing-block structure currently used for water supply would also be extended to sewerage and sewage treatment, both of which are presently charged at constant volumetric rates. Overall, this would make the tariff structure for water services significantly more progressive.

Table 17. **Wastewater Tariff Details for Households**

	Determination of sewerage (S) and sewage treatment (ST) charges
Australia	64% of pop'n: Fe: equal; PV (meter size no. of pedestals); 36% of pop'n: Fe: constant volumetric rate
Austria	Varies by water use, or house area
Belgium	Constant volumetric rate; fixed at regional level
Canada	Flat or (mostly) a given % of PWS charge
Czech Republic	Follows PWS bill
Denmark	Follows PWS bill; for connection fees, some separate schedules exist for rainwater collection and treatment
Finland	Follows PWS bill
France	Largely (or wholly) volumetric rate applied on water supplied
Germany	Follows PWS bill; some separate schedules exist for rainwater collection and treatment
Greece	(Athens) 40% of water bill
Hungary	Follows PWS bill
Iceland	(Reykjavik) Ff = 0.13-0.16% of PV
Ireland	Domestic charges have been consolidated into general taxation system
Italy	Constant volumetric rate on water use
Japan	Follows PWS bill, but with more "blocks"
Korea	Follows PWS tariff
Luxembourg	Fixed and equal: 42% of communes; fixed *per capita* (3%); follows PWS (43%); mixed approaches (12%).
Mexico	Based on level of water consumption
Netherlands	S: fixed per house (by utility); ST: pollution units (PUs): single people = 1PU; other households = 3 PUs
New Zealand	Ff: PV; metered; fixed + volumetric
Poland	Follows PWS bill
Portugal	S: by PV or quantity of water; ST: by quantity of water
Spain	Fixed charge per house, or volumetric rate
Sweden	Follows PWS bill
Turkey	Fixed % of PWS bill
UK:	
England and Wales	Follows PWS; metered: Fe + (90-100%) of PWS used
N. Ireland	Ff: PV
Scotland	Ff: PV
US	Nearly all constant volumetric rate + fixed or minimum charge

Notes:
– Ff   Flat fee.
– Fe   Fixed element.
– PV   Property value, rateable value of property, or some variant.
– Sewerage charges sometimes include stormwater disposal services, but detail on this is often unclear.
Sources: Ecotec (1996); Ecologic (1996-98); Ecologic (1997-98) and numerous publications or other documents supplied by and/or relating to individual countries, and assembled for this project.

The **Netherlands** is unique among OECD countries, in that household wastewater tariffs in that country are entirely based on non-volumetric charges. Interestingly, both economic theory and the pursuit of allocative economic efficiency could help justify the present Dutch policy, since some studies suggest that the long-run

---

Box 12.   Complex Wastewater Systems Can Lead to Problems

Wastewater collection and treatment in **Spain** is paid for through three types of charges. The discharge tax is levied by the Basin Authorities to the Municipalities and private water utilities for discharging into lakes and rivers. The sanitation tax is levied by the regional governments and local authorities to recover the costs of wastewater treatment, and municipal sewage charges. There are also other taxes, levied by the municipalities, to recover the costs of the municipal sewage network (Maestu, 1996: 14-15). A 1994 study calculated the average charge of Basin Authorities to Municipal Organisations at 0.48 Ptas per m^3 of water used.

In 1992, this highly complex discharge tax led to a situation in which only 1 600 million of the 6 500 million pesetas invoiced were actually received by the authorities. In consequence, subsidies from the central budget were needed to cover the operational costs of the Basin Authorities (Maestu, 1996: 16).

---

marginal cost of sewage services in the Netherlands is very small (Herrington, 1997b). However, in practice, the *Waterspoor* proposal discussed above is rationalised by the need to move towards full cost recovery, via the reduction of additional abstraction and pollution damage costs.

In 1995, **Denmark** also rejected the introduction of an otherwise rational two-part wastewater charge, although the:

> ... *possibility for dividing the [sewerage] charges into a fixed and variable part was given attention. The conclusion, however, was that efforts to reduce water consumption could be affected... and therefore the [separation] proposal was not to be recommended* (Miljoministeriet 1995, p. 73), (cited in Kragh, 1998; p. 36).

However, a Committee is currently analysing models for dividing sewerage charges (trade effluent charges) into fixed and variable parts. When this Committee has finished its work (1999), this situation may change.

On the other hand, only one-third of the urban population in **Australia** pay their sewerage and sewage treatment charges on a volumetric basis, and the volumetric share is typically very small (except in three utilities).[15] However, under the influence of the recent pricing reforms (which stress consumption-based charging), other water businesses in that country are now apparently reconsidering their position on this question.

Table 13 above provided information on wastewater pricing levels in those countries for which data are available. Table 18 also illustrates that, as with water usage charges, OECD countries apply a broad range of taxes and charges to their

Table 18. **Taxes and Levies in Household Wastewater Tariffs**[1]

Per cent

	Wastewater		
	VAT	Pollution charge	Other taxes
Australia	–	–	–
Austria	10	–	
Belgium	0	v	
Czech Republic	5	v	
Denmark	25	–	v[2]
Finland	22	–	–
France	5.5	v	
Germany	–	v	
Greece		–	
Hungary	12	–	–
Ireland	Domestic charges have been consolidated into general taxation system		
Italy	0		
Japan	5[3]	–	–
Korea	–	–	–
Luxembourg		–	
Netherlands	0	v	
Norway	22		
Poland		v	
Portugal	0	–[4]	
Spain	0	v	
Sweden	25	–[5]	–[5]
Switzerland	0	–	
Turkey	15	6	
UK:			
England and Wales	0	5	–
N. Ireland	0	5	–
Scotland	0	5	–

Note: A "blank" cell implies that data were not available; a cell with a "–" indicates "no charge"; and a cell with a "v" indicates that a charge is actually levied.

1. This Table lists taxes and other charges included or reflected in the water bills of domestic consumers. It lists charges levied in addition to "regular" wastewater charges (*e.g.* "sewer taxes").
2. Wastewater levy on pollution content of municipal discharge.
3. 5% consumption tax.
4. Planned.
5. Currently under formal discussion.
6. In metropolitan areas, new rules allow wastewater levies on pollution content, in proportion to deviations from "standard" discharge parameters.

domestic wastewater services. Again, VAT is the most common type of tax. **Finland, Sweden, Norway,** and **Denmark** charge VAT on all water services of more than 20 per cent, while at least seven countries zero-rate VAT on wastewater charges.

Pollution charges exist in eight countries, and are either planned or under discussion in two others. They generally recover less than the costs of the damages incurred. Only in **Germany** has a scheme been developed to explicitly provide incentives to improve the quality of discharges here, if consent conditions are not met, charges rise steeply. Again, when pollution charges are enhanced, the effect is to reduce the pollution damage that occurs, or to compensate those who are harmed by the discharges, and cost-recovery is achieved. Compensation payments also form part of the pollution permit procedures in some OECD countries (*e.g.* **Finland**).

Other distinctive taxes on wastewater exist in **France, Denmark,** and the **UK,** and are currently under discussion in **Sweden.** The **French** tax levied for FNDAE discussed earlier is used to finance some of the capital costs of rural water supply and wastewater services.

A new sewage levy was introduced in **Denmark** in January 1997 as part of the same tax reform programme as the water tax discussed earlier. It is payable on discharges to lakes, watercourses or the sea at a rate which depends on nitrogen, phosphorus, and organic matter content. Municipalities therefore recover some of their discharge costs by imposing a levy on households. Among other purposes, proceeds of the levy are used to support smaller waterworks having problems with polluted groundwater, again increasing overall cost recovery.

The **Swedish** government is currently considering the introduction of a separate discharge fee to act as an incentive for reducing pollution. The **UK** is also considering the use of economic instruments for pollution management, and their potential use in the management of abstractions. The government has recently issued consultation papers discussing the possibility of pollution charges or tradable permits for both types of charges. Increases in pollution charges above zero would, of course, oblige wastewater authorities to increase their revenues collected.

Some **US** utilities utilise seasonal tariffs for wastewater charging to better reflect marginal costs, with a large survey of US utilities in 1991 finding seven utilities out of 121 applying a seasonal component to their residential public wastewater tariffs (5.7 per cent of the total). Unaccountably, a 1997 survey of 121 utilities found none utilised seasonal wastewater tariffs [Lippiatt and Weber (1982), Markus (1993), and Raftelis Environmental Consulting Group (1998)].

7.2. Industrial sewage services provided by the public system

The volume and characteristics of industrial sewage vary considerably from one company to another. As a result, and unlike the situation for domestic wastewater, industrial water consumption levels do *not* represent a good proxy for industrial sewerage and sewage disposal costs. Thus, there have been trends (closely allied to the development of more cost-reflective water tariffs for industry) towards the separate and explicit identification of sewage, and towards the development of trade effluent prices and explicit charging mechanisms for industrial discharges to watercourses. The number of countries in which the costs of industrial sewage services are included in the prices of water services (or in general local taxes) has therefore been decreasing steadily. However, even where sewage services are separately identified on the bill, they are sometimes simply calculated as a percentage of the water bill (*e.g.* **Ireland** and **Poland**). Table 19 indicates the pricing structures for sewage services in various OECD countries, including any special tariffs that are applied.

Countries which do collect a specific sewage charge for the public supply of industrial wastewater services tend to apply a similar type of structure to that used for water pricing, albeit in a less sophisticated form. In the **US,** for instance, most sewage rates are based on uniform structures, with no seasonal volume adjustment. However, the introduction of extra load charges can be seen as an attempt to introduce prices based on marginal costs, especially when pollution charges reflect the additional treatment costs imposed on the system by each type of discharge.

Two-part sewage tariffs exist in **Australia, Denmark, Finland** and the **UK.** The fixed element can be based on the size and/or the value of the property, or on the meter size. In Australia for example, the fixed charge can be based on the value of the property, the meter size, or a discharge factor, and the volume charge can be based on the load of the pollutant.

In other countries (*e.g.* **Germany** and **Portugal**), both volumetric and fixed tariff elements are also used, but are generally mutually exclusive. In Portugal, for instance, wastewater collection and treatment costs are charged, either through an additional payment for each cubic meter of water supplied, or through a charge paid as part of the general municipal tax, and calculated as a function of the property price. The volume-based element is usually based on the volume of water consumed, since the volume of sewage is difficult to measure, and is not usually metered. In Germany, industrial water users can obtain a rebate if they are discharging a much smaller amount of (dirty) sewage than their water intake (for instance, if the water is used for cooling purposes).

One emerging issue which makes wastewater tariff structures more complicated than those for water supply is the issue of rainwater. So-called "combined" public sewerage services must treat both wastewater discharges by water users and rain water runoff (*e.g.* surface drainage and highway drainage). This sometimes creates a requirement to substantially increase the capacity of the sewers. In some countries (*e.g.* **Germany** and **Austria**), the connection charge is based either on the surface covered by the property, or the industrial estate as a proxy indicator of the related surface drained of rainwater. This charge is levied in order to cover the costs of treating rainwater. In other cases (*e.g.* the **UK**), surface and highway drainage charges are identified separately within the water bill; they are calculated as an added premium, and are generally not based on the surface drained (on the grounds that this would be too costly to administer).

Table 19. **Price Structure for Industrial Sewage Services from the Public System**

	SC	Tariff structure	FCR	ND	MC	DTS	Subs	Special tariffs
Australia	Yes	Fixed (various bases) + volume bases (various bases)	Yes	No	Yes	Yes	Yes	n.a.
Austria	Yes	Fixed (property size) or volume based (on water use)	Yes	No	n.a.	No	Yes	Partial rebates if less discharges than water used
Belgium	Yes	Depends on load	Yes	Yes	n.a.	Yes	No	n.a.
Canada	Yes	Treatment costs included in water bill if "no extra strength"	n.a.	n.a.	No	Yes	n.a.	n.a.
Czech Republic	Yes	n.a.	n.a.	n.a.	n.a.	n.a.	n.a.	n.a.
Denmark	Yes	Fixed (size of property) + Based on water volume	Yes	n.a.	n.a.	n.a.	No	n.a.
Finland	Yes	Paid within the water bill (volumetric + connection charges)	Yes	Yes	No	No	Negl.	n.a.
France	Yes	Percentage of water bill	n.a.	n.a.	n.a.	Yes	n.a.	Contract-based
Germany	Yes	Based on water volume or surface area	Yes	Yes	Yes	Yes	No	Rebates if less discharges than water used
Greece	Yes	Based on water volume	n.a.	n.a.	n.a.	n.a.	No	n.a.
Hungary	Yes	Based on water volume	n.a.	n.a.	n.a.	n.a.	Yes	n.a.
Ireland	No	Within water bill, not separate	n.a.	n.a.	n.a.	n.a.	Yes	Capital contributions
Italy	Yes	Based on water volume	No	No	Yes	Yes	Yes	n.a.
Japan	Yes	Based on water volume	No	n.a.	n.a.	Yes	Yes	n.a.
Korea	n.a.	Based on water volume	Yes	No	No	No	Yes	None
Luxembourg	Yes	Based on water volume	n.a.	n.a.	n.a.	n.a.	Yes	n.a.
Mexico	Yes	Based on water volume	No	n.a.	n.a.	n.a.	Yes	n.a.
Netherlands	Yes	Function of pollutant	Yes	n.a.	n.a.	Yes	Yes	n.a.
Poland	No	Percentage of water bill	n.a.	No	n.a.	Yes	Yes	n.a.
Portugal	Yes	Based on water volume or property size	n.a.	n.a.	n.a.	n.a.	Yes	n.a.
Spain	Yes	Recover operating and maintenance costs	Yes	No	n.a.	Yes	No	n.a.
Sweden	No	Fixed (size of meter or property) + volume based	Yes	No	Yes	Yes	n.a.	n.a.
Turkey	Yes	Based on water volume + connection charge	No	No	No	Yes	Yes	n.a.
UK (England and Wales)	Yes	Based on water volume; surface and highway drainage charges	Yes	Yes	n.a.	Yes	No	Large user tariffs
United States	Yes	Uniform structure, or increasing-block tariffs	n.a.	n.a.	n.a.	Yes	n.a.	No seasonal tariff

n.a.   Not available.
Notes:
SC: Is there a separate sewage charge?
Tariff structure: What are the types of tariff structures in place?
FCR: Is there full cost recovery? (*i.e.* are total revenues required to cover operating expenditure, plus depreciation, plus a return on capital employed?)
ND: Is non-discrimination a requirement? (*i.e.* do the tariffs for each customers group reflect the costs of the customer group concerned?)
MC: Is there any marginal cost pricing?
DTS: Do industrial customers have a different structure to other customers?
Subs.:   Are there any subsidies?
Special tariffs: Are there any special tariffs for industrial customers? This does *not* include extra strength trade effluent charges (see Table 20).

OECD 1999

7.3.   Trade effluent charges

In some cases, standard sewage charges can be difficult to distinguish from "special strength" charges, which are used to recover costs from any extra capacity built to treat industrial waste. These extra pollution charges levied by the service provider exist, for example, in **Belgium, Poland, Spain, Sweden** and the **UK**. In **Belgium** and the **Netherlands**, industrial users always pay a sewage charge per unit of pollution produced, which is equivalent to paying a trade effluent charge. In **Finland**, a similar charge is applied using a threshold: higher or lower tariffs are levied if wastewater quality considerably differs from the average.

It is only when "special strength" effluent charges are levied that the marginal costs of wastewater treatment for industrial discharges can be accurately reflected in the charging structure. So-called "trade effluent" charges are often specific to industrial users, since these are the heaviest polluters. They are the extra sewage charges paid to the service provider in order to reflect the additional costs created by the treatment of highly-polluted or difficult-to-treat effluents. This type of charge can also be levied by the environmental regulator as an economic instrument to regulate pollution flows, based on the Polluter Pays Principle. Table 20 indicates the current situation regarding trade effluent charges in OECD countries.

Service providers generally receive the proceeds of the trade effluent charge (*e.g.* **UK** and **US**). In **Austria**, industrial concerns can form "sewage treatment groups" with municipalities, and can set tariffs on the basis of the pollution loads discharged by each industrial user. This is the model adopted in **France** and **Spain**. In **France**, industrial users discharging to the public sewer have to pay a pollution charge which varies according to the pollution load of their discharge. The pollution charge is collected by the service provider through the water bill, and then paid to the River Basin Agencies. The Agencies cannot initiate the construction of new works themselves, but they can provide subsidies to various classes of water consumer.

Some countries, such as **Hungary** and **Portugal,** have not introduced a trade effluent charging regime as yet, but are planning to do so in the near future. In many countries, the introduction of extra-strength charges has been piecemeal, and is usually decided at the local level (*e.g.* **Canada, Denmark, Ireland** and **Japan**). In Canada, there is no well-established regime of trade effluent charges. However, if industries make extra strength discharges, additional fees can (in a limited number of cases) be negotiated as part of the contract between the industry and the respective municipality. In Denmark, additional trade effluent charges have been introduced by some municipalities, but others have been reluctant to do so for fear of losing industrial users, or due to the high monitoring costs entailed. In other countries (*e.g.* **Greece**), no trade effluent charging regime seems likely to appear in the near future.

Table 20. **Trade Effluent Charges**

	Strength charge?	Levied by?	Based on?	Specifications
Australia	Yes	Service providers	List of pollutants	Levied by certain providers only
Austria	Yes	Some municipalities	(e.g.) COD, above a given volume of water used	Applies everywhere
Belgium	Yes	Municipalities – Fund	Pollution unit, based on industry factor	Some charges on water temperature
Canada	Yes	Large municipalities	Percentage added to water bill	Levied by certain providers only
Czech Republic	Discharge charges	n.a.	n.a.	n.a.
Denmark	Yes	Municipalities	Volume and pollution control	Levied by certain providers only
Finland	Yes	Municipalities	Volume + pollution content (extra strength)	n.a.
France	Yes	River Basin Agencies	Allocated pollution loads by industry. Pollution parameters	Charge varies with pollution location; applies everywhere
Germany	Yes	Länder or municipality	Pollution unit by pollution parameter	n.a.
Greece	No	n.a.	n.a.	n.a.
Hungary	No	n.a.	n.a.	n.a.
Ireland	Yes	Local authorities	Volume related	Levied by certain localities only
Italy	Yes	Municipalities	Quantity and quality criteria	n.a.
Japan	Yes	n.a.	n.a.	Levied by certain municipalities only
Korea	Discharge charges	n.a.	n.a.	n.a.
Luxembourg	Discharge charges	n.a.	n.a.	n.a.
Netherlands	Yes	Water Boards	Charge per pollution unit	Large industrials are closely monitored
Poland	Discharge charges	n.a.	n.a.	n.a.
Portugal	No	n.a.	n.a.	n.a.
Spain	Yes	River Basin Agencies invest in treatment	Pollution content in population equivalent	Applies everywhere
Sweden	Yes	Municipalities	Pollution content	Contract based
Turkey	Yes	Municipalities	Fixed charge plus pollution content	Applies everywhere
UK (England and Wales)	Yes	Water companies	MOGDEN" formula (pollution content)	Varies
US	Yes	Water network	Pollution content	Monitoring expenses

n.a.   Not available.

OECD 1999

Trade effluent charges usually depend on the metered volume of pollutants and pollution contents. Some countries, such as **Belgium** and the **Netherlands,** charge according to pollution units, which are calculated based on certain formulae for each type of pollutant. In Belgium, a pollution factor is calculated for each type of industrial activity, and the wastewater charge in a given year is set proportional to the charge paid in the previous year. The law was recently changed to give additional incentives to polluters to reduce their discharges of heavy metals.

In **France,** a charge is levied on the 8 types of pollutants deemed to be the most dangerous and difficult to treat (heavy metals, phosphorus, soluble salts, etc.). The charge is calculated as a function of pollution produced in a normal day, and during the period of maximum activity. River Basin Agencies have considerable flexibility in determining pollution fees and some agencies do not charge for certain categories (*e.g.* there is no charge for soluble salts in the Adour-Garonne Basin).

In other cases (*e.g.* the **UK**), the charging formula reflects the costs to the water treatment companies of treating a particular effluent; the pollution content of the effluent may be defined, for example, on the basis of chemical oxygen demand (COD), or the level of suspended solids. Other factors can affect the value of the charge, such as the location of the pollution (with, for instance, the definition of "sensitive zones" in **France** by each River Basin Agency) or the type of receiving body (*i.e.* lake, river, estuary, etc.).

Given that trade effluents can create a risk for the wastewater treatment system as a whole (due to unexpected variations in strength characteristics and volumes), some service providers have introduced "capacity charges" for trade effluent, in order to incorporate the value of this risk into the charging system (such as the East of Scotland Water Authority, **UK,** or in Melbourne, **Australia**).

7.4. Direct discharges

In countries where sewage service costs have risen (*e.g.* due to higher environmental standards), and have led to price increases, industrial users have increasingly questioned whether the public sewer system represents the most cost-effective means of discharging their sewage. As a result, there is some evidence of a greater use of self-treatment and effluent re-use by industry. It is also likely that this has impacted on the production processes used by industry, to ensure that the costs of disposing and treating this effluent are kept to a minimum.

Discharge controls are imposed on direct discharges, both those which do not go through the public sewer, and those which emanate from the public sewerage and sewage treatment system, following treatment. The proceeds of these discharge controls always go either to the government (*e.g.* to cover administration costs or to provide revenues for the protection of the environment) or to an environmental fund, since no service provider is involved.

The most common form of discharge control is linked to permit procedures: in order to discharge directly back into the river or the aquifer, industrial users (and other dischargers) usually need a permit. Most countries regulate the quality of waters which can be directly discharged, and breaking these quality standards leads to the imposition of fines. This can be seen as an alternative to a formal regime of discharge charges. In **Ireland,** for instance, charges are imposed in the licensing process, and fines for non-compliance or illegal releases can be levied (firms may also be held responsible for reimbursing the costs incurred by local authorities in clean-up or remediation). In **Austria,** industrial dischargers must comply with discharge standards, and separate regulations have been promulgated for about 70 different sectors. In **Korea,** if standards for direct discharges are violated, the industrial discharger must pay an additional charge which depends on the degree of violation of the standard and the amount of wastewater discharged.

These systems are relatively "piece-meal", however, and cannot always be enforced in a comprehensive manner. This is one reason why some OECD countries have introduced formal discharge charge regimes, calculated in various ways. In the **Netherlands,** for example, charges for discharges into the main watercourses which are directly administered by the State, based either on pollution loads estimated using input-output models for each industrial sector, or – for the most significant pollutants – based on metering the quality and quantity of effluent.[16] It is only for the largest polluters that the quality and quantity of the effluent are metered. For smaller polluters, pollution loads are estimated using input-output models for each industrial sector. In **Mexico,** discharge charges were recently introduced (1997), and can vary according to the receiving body, the location of the discharge, the volume, and the pollution content. If a significant effort is made by a company to improve pre-treatment, a discount may be granted. In **Poland,** industrial dischargers must pay fees for actual wastewater discharges, and fines for non-compliance are also imposed.

In the **Czech Republic,** charges for wastewater discharged into surface waters were introduced in 1979, and the charge is equivalent to the running costs of a wastewater treatment plant that would remove the pollution under consideration, measured in pollution units by type of pollutant. A surcharge is also imposed, in order to take account of adverse effects on receiving waters. When the polluter starts building a wastewater treatment plant, he is allowed to delay the payment of 60 per cent of these charges until construction is completed, so long as the project is completed in reasonable time. If there are delays, he has to pay the full amount of deferred charges, with penalties.

In **Finland,** water protection charges are imposed on heavy polluters on a case-by-case basis by the Water Rights Court, and revenues from these charges are "earmarked" for water protection activities. In addition, there is a fish management charge levied on any polluters whose activities might have an adverse impact on fish stocks. These charges are not, however, related to actual pollution content, and charge levels are too small to offer any incentives for reducing pollution levels. In **France,** pollution charges apply to direct discharges, and are levied by the River Basin Agencies. These charges are calculated on the basis of a pollution load defined by industry, modified by a "zone factor". Similar calculations are carried out in **Germany,** but there is a 75 per cent reduction in the charge, if the standards contained in the regulations (expressed as "Best Available Technique") are met.

Table 21. **Discharge Charges**

	Charge?	Levied by?	Based on pollution content?	Fines?
Austria	No	d.n.a	d.n.a	d.n.a
Belgium	Yes	State Envtl. Fund	Pollution content or volume (if > 500 m³)	n.a.
Czech Republic	Yes	n.a.	Pollution content	Yes
Denmark	No	n.a.	d.n.a.	n.a.
Finland	Yes	State	No: case-by-case basis; largest polluters only	Yes
France	Yes	River Basin Agency	Charges per pollutant vary according to user; regional variations	Yes
Germany	Yes	Länder/Municipalities	Pollution content (definition of pollution units for each pollutant)	Yes
Greece	No	d.n.a	d.n.a	n.a.
Hungary	No	d.n.a	d.n.a	n.a.
Ireland	Yes	Local authority	n.a.	Yes
Italy	No	d.n.a.	d.n.a.	n.a.
Korea	Yes	Region	Pollution content (definition of pollution units for each pollutant)	Yes
Mexico	Yes	n.a.	Receiving body, location, volume and pollution content. Discount if improved treatment	Yes
Netherlands	Yes	State	Pollution per population equivalent Input-output model, for largest polluters, quality and quantity metered	Yes
Poland	Yes	Environment Fund	Fees vary according to pollutant, industrial sector and receiving body	Yes
Spain	Yes	River Basin Agency	Based on pollution content calculated per population equivalent	n.a.
Turkey	Yes	State/Municipalities	Pollution content in some municipalities	Yes
UK (England and Wales)	n.a.	n.a.	n.a.	Yes
US	n.a.	n.a.	n.a.	Yes

n.a. Not available.   d.n.a Does not apply.

In **Sweden,** the government proposed (1988) that a Parliamentary Committee develop a new tax on water use and/or discharge. At the moment, the Swedish Board of Agriculture is studying options for a fee system for nutrient (phosphorous and nitrogen) surpluses (*i.e.* losses to water and air) and the over-use of nutrients.

Table 21 provides an overview of the current situation in some OECD countries with respect to discharge charges.

OECD 1999

Chapter 8
Subsidies

When the principle of "full cost recovery" is not completely implemented, a wedge may develop between full and actual costs (see the Annex for a more detailed discussion). This wedge is sometimes referred to as a "subsidy". It can take several forms in practice, not all of which are necessarily "bad" for either the environment or the economy. Nor are all of these various forms of direct relevance to this report. For example, when a private individual is paid a sum of money by the government for water services provided to the public-at-large, this is sometimes called a "subsidy", with all the negative implications that this word carries. However, two points are worth noting about such payments.

First, if they are truly payments on behalf of *public* water management goals (*i.e.* the benefits do not accrue to the recipient at a personal level), economic theory suggests that they may simply be payments for the internalisation of external management benefits – not "subsidies" at all. Examples here include the countryside management and flood control benefits often ascribed to the agricultural sector.

Second, and perhaps more importantly for this report, if these payments do not affect the total price actually paid for water services, they may be relevant to the water management problem more broadly, but they are not necessarily relevant to a discussion of water pricing *per se*. For example, a payment for a water management service provided by a farmer may have little to do with the price of water services actually used by that farmer.

On the other hand, some types of payment, and some price exemptions, *are* relevant for the water pricing problem. For example, subsidies are often given for the construction of water infrastructure, or for its operation. Such subsidies benefit (directly or indirectly) all users, by indirectly reducing the total costs of water services.

Subsidies to infrastructure development and maintenance can have two main consequences: *i)* they can lead to a supply-oriented approach to water management, with important demand-side options being downgraded; and *ii)* they can lead to relatively low unit prices for water. At low prices, consumption will increase; pressure will grow to increase supplies even further; and infrastructure facilities will be poorly maintained. The end result will be higher use rates for water, coupled with either degradation of the infrastructure or ever-increasing public subsidies to maintain that infrastructure in an acceptable state.

Another form of subsidy which exists in the water service sector, but which is more difficult to quantify, is the uncompensated environmental degradation associated with overuse of water (or with water pollution). These "environmental subsidies" result from a failure to internalise the external costs associated with water use. Given that water users rarely pay for either the opportunity cost of the water they use, or for the pollution they generate, these users may be said to be subsidised by society-at-large.

Water price subsidies do not necessarily involve the government. They may also be provided by one group of consumers to another, or from some other economic group (*e.g.* producers) to another (*e.g.* consumers). This is know as "cross-subsidisation", and its impact on the achievement of economic, environmental, or social goals can be just as problematic as subsidies received directly from the government.

Some pricing subsidies are given for social reasons – based on the premise that water is such a fundamental element of life that it should not carry a price. The difficulty with this approach is that all consumers of water, not just those consumers who have difficulty paying the water rates, receive a signal from the economic system that encourages over-investment in infrastructure facilities, and over-consumption of the water resource itself. Experience generally indicates that there are often more efficient ways of achieving social objectives of this type than direct subsidies (*e.g.* raising income support levels, or targeting special water tariffs to those in particular need) (OECD, 1998*b*).

All subsidies represent a financial burden either on the government or on other sectors which may be cross-subsidising particular consumers, and most provide exactly the wrong signals needed to encourage consumers to conserve water. Another side-effect is that subsidies often do not even achieve their intended economic objectives. Even where economic subsidies are designed with environmental objectives in mind, the long-term results may not be positive for the environment. For example, subsidies which encourage new irrigation techniques may also lead to an increased scale of economic activity, eventually offsetting any beneficial environmental effects of these new technologies.

Most OECD countries currently ascribe to the *principle* of "full cost recovery" in the provision of water services. However, some OECD countries are more advanced than others in the actual *implementation* of this principle. A summary of the degree of "cost coverage" currently being achieved in selected OECD countries in the water sector is provided in the remainder of this chapter.

8.1. Subsidies to household water supply

In **Canada**, approximately C$ 3.3 billion is raised annually through municipal water rates, but the additional annual costs for the operation, maintenance, and improvement of the water and wastewater system have been estimated to be C$ 4.5 billion between 1993 and 2003, suggesting a C$ 1.2 billion subsidy per annum (Tate and Lacelle, 1995).

In **Norway**, the building of new or upgraded infrastructure is also subsidised by state authorities – at a rate of 7.3 per cent in 1995. In principle, municipalities are supposed to set the price of water at a level where the revenues equal the costs of water supply. However, municipalities are not restricted from subsidising the water supply if they want to lower the general tax-level (Sjoholt, 1996).

Italy has a long history of public involvement in the financing of public water works. Until the early 1980s, water services had been provided virtually free, but a worsening of water quality, overexploitation of underground catchments, as well as growing budgetary constraints, each contributed to some reorganisation of these patterns. Charges have increased significantly, and are expected to continue to do so in the future. However, municipalities still face considerable political constraints in setting the level of their charges to reflect cost structures. As a result, they remain largely dependent on subsidies to cover investment and maintenance costs, with an estimated 70 per cent of the capital expenditure for water supply still being financed by public budgets (Massarutto, 1993). In absolute numbers, approximately 3 billion ECU have been transferred via grants or favourable loans for water supply purposes during the last decade. Furthermore, an additional 10-25 billion ECU is deemed to be necessary to meet the investment needs of maintaining and improving the current water supply infrastructure (Massarutto, 1996: 14).

Denmark's counties and municipalities are allowed to subsidise waterworks, principally for investment purposes, as well as to subsidise operating costs in some circumstances. The extent of this subsidisation is not known, but is estimated to be limited (Wallach, 1996).

In the **Netherlands**, the perception is that the water resource base is slowly degrading (*i.e.* an "environmental subsidy" exists), with the result that water prices are expected to have to increase by about 10 per cent annually, at least over the short-term. The extra revenues raised from these increases will be used to finance further investments into preventive measures against point source pollution, as well as the removal of (non-point) nitrates, pesticides, and chemicals. These increasing fees for investment purposes, however, still constitute a cross-subsidisation to the main polluters (mostly in agriculture) (van den Bergen, 1993: 5).

A few OECD countries have long traditions of public supply and subsidisation of domestic water services, but are actively working towards the reduction or elimination of these subsidies. In the **Czech Republic,** for example, drinking water supply was ensured by regional state-run enterprises before 1992, and was subsidised from the state budget by more than 2 billion Ck. Through a step-by-step increase, (implemented since 1994), prices now cover the production costs of water services, so subsidisation of the *operations* of water companies is rare.[17] *Investments* in the water sector are still supported by the state budget (to a maximum of 80 per cent of the investment cost), although this too is being reduced. Another subsidy is given in the form of interest-free loans. Overall, state financial support for water supply represented 1.4 billion Ck in 1995, and 1.7 billion Ck in 1996. However, taking the inflation rate into account, state financial support in the Czech Republic has actually been declining in recent years (Pavlík, 1996: 2).

Since 1985, the **Spanish** water supply system has also been undergoing transformation from a situation where water was considered to be a public good, to one where costs are increasingly being internalised. Currently, an estimated 50 per cent of infrastructure costs for the supply of water is provided via subsidies from various sources (Maestu, 1996). In 16 per cent of municipalities, operational costs are also subsidised (Maestu, 1996: 18). Although the water supply agencies and Municipal Authorities have to pay a volumetric charge to the Basin Authorities such that the revenues cover the Basin Authorities' capital and operational costs, the Basin Authorities still experienced a deficit of 5.4 billion pesetas in 1994. This was covered through subsidies from the central budget.[18]

In **Ireland,** the capital costs of providing public water supplies are entirely met by the central government, with substantial assistance being provided by the European Union, from Structural or Cohesion Funds. A 1996 report concluded that the water and sewage charges levied in 1995 only covered about 75 per cent of the costs of operating and maintaining water and sewage services, representing a 25 per cent subsidy through under-pricing of services (KPMG Consultants, 1996: 41).

Even when water supply services are fully privatised, and the responsible suppliers are charged on a "full cost recovery" basis, some subsidies can still be found in terms of preferential tax treatment. This is the case in the **UK**, where water companies have to cover both their operational and infrastructural costs from the charges taken for their services. Although they are also generally liable to pay corporation taxes, some tax relief in the form of capital allowances is granted for "qualifying capital expenditures". There are also tax exemptions for water consumers, since most water supply is not subject to VAT (see Chapter 5 of this report, as well as Zabel and Orman, 1996).

The results of one study which estimated how increased domestic water prices necessary to move toward "full cost recovery" would affect household incomes are presented in Table 22. This study examined the ratio of average water charges to average household incomes, under the assumptions that: *i)* water services were to be provided for the first time to a "greenfield" site in a hypothetical urban area

Table 22. **Effects of "Full Cost Recovery" on Household Incomes
in Selected OECD Countries**

Per cent

	Water charges as a proportion of household incomes	
	Existing water	Full cost tariffs recovery
Portugal	0.5	2.8
Greece	0.4	2.1
Ireland	0.3	1.9
Spain	0.4	1.6
France	1.1	1.5
UK (England and Wales)	1.2	1.3
Germany	1.0	1.2
Denmark	0.8	0.9
Korea	0.6	0.9

Sources: Based on Ecotec (1996), Final Report, and cited in OECD (1999c).

(with primary and secondary wastewater treatment); and *ii*) there were to be full cost recovery of all direct economic costs, both operating and capital. As would be expected, the results indicate the need to raise water prices considerably in the EU "Cohesion Fund" countries, whereas the more mature EU economies would experience relatively small price increases, reflecting the relatively low subsidies currently in effect.

8.2. Subsidies to industrial water supply

Subsidies are sometimes given directly to industrial users for improvements to their water abstraction or treatment capacities. In **Canada,** for example, municipalities often offer special "promotional" water rates to industry, seeking to enhance the local economic base through these subsidies. The necessary infrastructural measures for the provision of water have also been accomplished through large subsidy programmes (Tate and Rivers, 1990; Tate and Scharf, 1995).

In **Norway,** subsidies are given for the building of new (or the upgrading of existing) water plants. In **Greece,** a minimum of 35 per cent of necessary infrastructure investments is automatically granted to each company by the central Government. **EU** funds may also contribute to the building of water and wastewater treatment plants in **Greece, Hungary,** and **Portugal.**

Another common example of subsidies to industries are loan reductions for investments in water and wastewater treatment plants. Such subsidies exist in **Austria,** for example, where subsidised loans are available for water and wastewater projects.

119

In **France**, industrial users can receive subsidies directly from the River Basin Agencies, when they are building water and wastewater treatment plants for direct abstractions and discharges. However, these funds come from the other users of the water system, via pollution and abstraction charges, so they are more appropriately interpreted as a form of redistribution, than as subsidies. Various assessments have indicated that cost coverage for domestic and industrial water services in France is approximately 95 per cent (February, 1999).

In **Denmark**, municipal and private water works generally seek to cover the full amount of capital and operational costs via water tariffs and charges. However, there are some examples of quantity discounts for industrial users. In terms of the tax on water consumption recently introduced as part of the green tax reform, industrial water users can also deduct this tax on water consumption from their VAT proceeds (Wallach 1996; Andersen 1996).

Table 10 above also provided an overview of the existing situation in OECD countries with respect to the existence (and type) of subsidies offered to industrial water consumers using the public water supply system.

8.3. Subsidies to irrigation water supply

Most countries' water pricing policies are solidly embedded within their water codes or irrigation development acts. Commonly, these various pieces of legislation establish how water project costs should be evaluated, capitalised, assigned to different users, and recovered over time. However, there is ample evidence across OECD countries to suggest that agricultural water prices have traditionally failed to raise enough revenues to meet even the modest recoveries which have been established by law.

Until quite recently, the fact that farmers were using water at subsidised rates remained largely unchallenged by other elements of society. Legislative bodies and governments often saw the development of irrigation as a means of promoting food production, of developing land, or of making use of hydraulic works for other purposes, such as hydropower generation or flood control. As long as water resources remained reasonably available for competing users, the fact that farmers used large volumes themselves, occasionally to grow low-value crops, did not face significant social opposition.

Where pressures to reduce subsidies to irrigation water usage are lacking, irrigation pricing systems tend to evolve in two stages. First, water agencies begin to charge farmers "reasonable" prices, usually meaning charges that are levied in accordance with some fraction of farmers' net returns or "ability-to-pay". At this point, charges start to deviate significantly from water supply costs. After a few decades, irrigation water pricing policies then evolve towards the second stage, whose main characteristic is that different farmers operating in the same region end up paying widely differing prices, even though they are (in principle) subject to the same "ability-to-pay" considerations. For example, Wahl (1989) showed that across 17 **US** Federal Water Projects, one could encounter farmers for which the ratio of "willingness-to-pay" to "ability-to-pay" for irrigation water, ranged from 51.0 to 1.9. Examples from **Spain** and other countries illustrate this same evolution. It is clear that such a system is not only inefficient, but also highly inequitable.

The water charges paid by farmers in almost all OECD countries do not cover the capital costs of irrigation water supply, and it is only in a few that the full O&M costs are covered (Box 13). In **Turkey,** for example, it is estimated that farmers' payments in the past only covered about 40 per cent of the previous years' O&M costs, partly because inflation was ignored in setting rates for the new year, and partly because the actual collection of water charges from farmers tended to be quite low. However, beginning in 1993, the Government began to accelerate the transfer of large-scale irrigation facilities to local users, primarily in an effort to reduce this financial burden on the public sector. The result has been a sharp increase in O&M cost recovery rates (for example, collection rates have increased from less than 54 per cent under the previous arrangements, to an average of 90 per cent under the water user associations). In theory, water charges are also required to include the recovery of capital costs, and over a period not exceeding 50 years. In practice, however, no interest is charged on capital amounts, and amortisation charges (once adopted) are not generally subjected to changes due to inflation. Allowances are also made on the basis of the repayment capacity of the farmer, on the geographic location of the farm, and on the amount of the original investment. The net result is that considerable capital subsidies still exist.

Box 13.   Subsidies and Expanding Irrigation Systems

In **Portugal,** a substantial new irrigation project is currently under construction (the Aqueleva project in Guadiana Basin), which is to be completed in 2024, and is estimated will expand Portugal's total irrigation area by between 110 000 and 200 000 hectares. Considering the size of the project, it is very unlikely that the final beneficiaries would ever be able to make positive economic returns, should they be required to pay for all of the capital costs directly attributable to them. Currently, there is intense debate in Portugal about how the operating and maintenance (O&M) and capital costs of this major new project should be distributed among the various user sectors. From this example, it can be seen that periods of expansion in irrigation infrastructure are often not very compatible with the goal of implementing "full cost recovery" prices.

121

A similar transformation has been occurring in **Mexico**. Although farmers' contri butions there accounted for 95 per cent of the costs of irrigation water supply in 1950, this figure had fallen significantly in recent years, so that by 1990, only 37 per cent of these costs were being covered. Partly as a result of this poor cos recovery rate, the government instituted a programme in 1990 to transfer manage ment responsibility from the National Water Commission to water users, in the form of irrigation modules operated by user associations. By 1996, over 91 per cent o publicly irrigated land had been transferred, and the modules were estimated to be running at 80 per cent of financial self-sufficiency (O&M costs only).

Despite relatively high irrigation water charges in **Greece**, Greek farmers oper ating in publicly-developed irrigation units do not fully cover even their O&M costs This is largely because irrigation projects are considered to contribute to the devel opment of rural regions, and as such are often given government financial assis tance. A noteworthy exception is that of a public (albeit financially autonomous) company operating in Crete which supplies water to both farmers and households water. This company charges rates that are set in line with the particular O&M costs incurred in servicing each type of client. Furthermore, for the 60 per cent of all Greek irrigation acreage that is under private control, all costs are covered by the private sector.

The price charged for irrigation by **Spanish** Basin Authorities, which charge local irrigators for the abstraction of water from public water supplies, are similarly insuf ficient to cover operating costs. In 1994, the shortfalls[19] amounted to 5.4 billion pesetas, which had to be covered by subsidies from the central budget (OECD, 1997).

In **France**, the fact that farmers are heavily subsidised to invest in irrigation equipment offsets (at least to some extent) the effects of increased water prices, which act as deterrents to further agricultural water abstractions. These incentives are reinforced by the **EU**'s Common Agricultural Policy, which rewards those farmers with installed irrigation equipment more generously than those without it (Rainelli and Vermesch, 1998).

While not a direct subsidy, some countries (including **Sweden** and **Canada**) allow farmers to directly abstract groundwater for free, although licenses or other administrative permissions may need to be obtained for such activities.

In the **Western US**, the subsidisation of agricultural water and irrigation activities is particularly well-documented for water projects that reclaim arid and semi-arid land (for example, see Wahl, 1989: Chapter 2; and Harden, 1996). The fed eral government has been involved in financing and building water projects in this area since 1902. Under the federal law which governs reclamation water projects, agricultural irrigators can receive three types of financial assistance: *i*) interest-free financing of a project's construction costs; *ii*) shifting of part or all of their repayment obligations to other beneficiaries of a project; iii) relief of part or all of their repayment obligations through specific legislation in special circumstances, such as economic hardship or drought.

As of September 1994, US$16.9 billion of the federal investment in water projects was considered to be reimbursable by the beneficiaries of these programmes, of which agricultural irrigators had received US$7.1 billion. However, as a result of special repayment relief, the amount owed by irrigators was reduced to US$3.4 billion (i.e. 47 per cent of the irrigators' share of total construction costs). Of the 133 projects assessed by a recent government report (GAO, 1996), 15 projects relieved irrigators of 50 per cent or more of their repayment obligation. In 41 projects, irrigation assistance and charge-offs accounted for 70 per cent or more of the costs allocated to irrigation, and 39 projects were reported where irrigation assistance and charge-offs accounted for 10 per cent or less of the costs allocated to irrigation.

Traditionally, **Canada's** water supply policy has resulted in heavily subsidised irrigation supply (with some estimates indicating subsidies amounting to 90 per cent of supply costs). Although Canada's provinces are in charge of setting agricultural water prices, it was only the three driest ones that were charging farmers water rates by 1988. Tighter federal budgets, together with an inability to raise enough revenues, have prompted many agencies to increase the use and levels of agricultural water charges in recent years.

In addition to the process of reforming irrigation water subsidies currently taking place in many OECD Member countries, some have also begun imposing taxes on water use. However, agricultural water consumers are often exempt from these taxes, or are offered preferential rates. Thus, taxation of agricultural water is common in **Germany,** but the revenues are often passed back to the farmers, either through compensation for restrictions on fertiliser use in vulnerable areas, or as tax rebates (up to 90 per cent) for farmers who are placed in financial difficulty by the tax. Similarly, in the **Netherlands**, farmers extracting less than 100 000 m^3 per annum are exempt from the groundwater tax. Despite this tax exemption, overall the Dutch agricultural sector contributes more revenues to water management than is actually spent in its direct benefit, with a discrepancy of about 5 per cent.

As of 1995, all licensed uses of water in **Portugal** are subject to a tax that is directly proportional to the amount of water used (and to the economic value of that water for each specific sector), and inversely proportional to water availability. While the legislation will be implemented gradually for most sectors until 1999 (when 100 per cent will be paid), agricultural withdrawals for irrigation purposes will be fully exempted for the first five years (Correia et al., 1997: 508-509).

The lowering of subsidies to agriculture seems to be facilitated where control over the irrigation system passes from public to private control. For example, the operation and maintenance of the main irrigation equipment (still in state ownership) costs the **Czech Republic** government about 100 million Ck annually in direct subsidies. To cover the costs of providing the irrigation water itself (operational costs), the state-run water organisation receives an additional 25 million Ck annually. As with subsidies to domestic water consumption, these systems are now being reduced, and since 1992, no further subsidies have been given for the construction of new irrigation facilities. With the intended privatisation of the main irrigation equipment, this subsidy scheme is expected to eventually be completely stopped (Pavlík, 1996: 6-8).

New Zealand successfully followed a similar process of privatisation of the irrigation system, and removed all subsidies to irrigation in 1988. Before this, the majority of costs for the development, maintenance and operation of irrigation systems had been funded by the government, even after including delivery costs and water charges to irrigators. Today, all irrigation systems have been privatised, and must be financed from private sources.

Although the **Australian** federal government (under the powers of the Council of Australian Governments) has made progress in agreeing guidelines for the implementation of full-cost recovery principles, special provisions have been made regarding the recovery of irrigation supply costs. As a result, while the implementation of the new agricultural water pricing systems so far have resulted in water charge increases of 30-35 per cent, it was estimated that as much as a 250 per cent increase might be required for full cost recovery.

8.4. Subsidies to sewerage and sewage disposal

Subsidies also exist in the provision of sewage treatment facilities and services through the application of "below full cost" rates. For domestic and industrial users of the public water system, wastewater charges are often insufficient to cover the full costs of providing these services. For agricultural users, although irrigation run-off can be quite polluting (particularly where minerals are leached), there are generally no facilities in place to reduce this "environmental subsidy".

Domestic sewage

Subsidies to domestic sewerage treatment and disposal are common, particularly where these services are traditionally paid for out of the public budget. This is the case in **Italy,** for example, where approximately 7 billion ECU have been transferred via grants and favourable loans for sewerage and sewage treatment purposes over the last decade (Massarutto, 1996: 16).

Sewer construction, operation, and maintenance are the responsibility of municipal governments in the **Netherlands.** In the past, there were several subsidies available for speeding up the connection of wastewater discharges to the sewer network, and to the Publicly-owned Treatment Works (PTWs). Apart from a general flow of state money to municipalities (the "Municipality Fund"), which is used to finance a wide variety of municipal tasks, as of 1993, there were no programmes in force to transfer money for the operation, maintenance or expansion of the sewerage/water treatment systems. Current policy requires municipalities to strive for 100 per cent coverage of sewerage management expenses from their own resources, preferably by levying a sewer tax. The net result is that, only in "dedicated soil protection areas" are some (very limited) subsidies still available (van den Bergen, 1993: 6).

In **Norway,** the costs of wastewater treatment are estimated to be 12 per cent higher than those paid into the waste and wastewater fee, resulting in a 12 per cent subsidy to households from the municipalities (Sjoholt, 1996).

Switzerland is currently discussing the reform of its system of subsidising the construction of sewerage and wastewater treatment from the central budget. To date, subsidies to the Cantons have ranged between 15-45 per cent of construction costs. Despite drastically reduced contributions from the central budget to future projects in this area, outstanding obligations of the central budget still amount to 1 370 million SFR (Eidgenössisches Departement des Innern, 1996).

Although the **Czech Republic** no longer subsidises *operating* costs, subsidies for *investments* covered 77 per cent of costs in 1995. This amounted to 1.5 billion Ck in 1995, and will reach 1.0 billion Ck in 1996 (Pavlík, 1996: 2). The main source of financial support is the State Environmental Fund, administered by the Ministry of Environment.

Because large regional inequalities exist in the Czech Republic, and because the municipalities do not yet have enough financial resources for required investments in network renewal and/or enlargement, existing subsidy schemes will still be necessary for the immediate future. To meet water quality requirements for public water supply, as well as to improve the quality of water in catchment areas for water abstraction, the subsidised construction and modernisation of waste water treatment plants and sewerage facilities is seen to be necessary, from both a public health and an environmental perspective.

In **Spain** as well, the continued subsidisation of wastewater investments is perceived to be necessary in order to meet environmental and social objectives. To meet the objectives set out by European Union Directive 271/91, an estimated 1.9 trillion pesetas (12.101 billion ECU) of investments in new connections and infrastructural improvements will be required (Maestu, 1996: 4).

In **Australia,** the "full cost recovery" objective regarding constructing and maintaining water discharge and sewerage systems is gradually being achieved. A survey of metropolitan areas conducted by the Australian Resource Management Committee of Australia and New Zealand shows that Melbourne Water achieved full cost recovery in 1993-94, and subsidies in other districts comprised only a small proportion of the real costs of service provision. However, the existing negative environmental externalities will still require large new investments in the future In 1990, the Australian Water Resources Council estimated that new investments o over A\$ 2.5 billion would be required for urban sewerage treatment assets in orde to provide limited improvements in nutrient removal.

While the **Danish** national tax on wastewater, implemented in 1997, wil go a long way towards covering wastewater costs, reportedly certain (pollution intensive) industries (fishing, cellulose production, sugar-production, and certair chemical industries) will be partly exempted from this tax (Wallach, 1996).

Industrial sewage

The pricing of wastewater services for industrial users is generally based or accounting principles, which aim at covering some fraction of the *historic* costs of pro viding these services. However, charging systems based on historic costs will not typically generate sufficient revenues to finance *current* investment needs. There is a considerable backlog of investment needs in wastewater treatment capacity in OECD countries. For this reason, even if sewage tariffs are set to recover operating and maintenance costs, they would be insufficient to cover future investment costs. This is particularly true in **Japan,** where the current sewerage connection rate is low by OECD standards, and in some **EU** countries, where the implementation of the Urban Waste Water Treatment Directive (91/271/EEC) has led to considerable investment needs in order to comply with more stringent standards. In **Ireland,** for example, where charges for water and sewerage services have traditionally been low, local authorities have recently started asking industrial users to make capital contributions to new investments in wastewater capacities, in order to improve the financial self-sufficiency of the service.

In **Canada,** industrial plants mostly discharge their waste waters directly to surface waters. As shown by a recent survey, between 50 and 60 per cent of these discharges occur in an untreated form, and just over 40 per cent of discharges are treated by primary mechanical methods. As reported by Tate and Scharf (1995), current practices have succeeded in minimising private sector costs, but have also created serious and persistent water pollution problems, despite very expensive regulatory efforts (1995: 43). The money required to regulate the environmental externalities of industrial wastewater discharges is generated from the general state budget, and not from the polluters themselves.

In **Australia,** there is generally full-cost recovery of sewage costs, and more consideration is being given to the environmental effects of disposal. Large sewage disposers face volume-based charges and extra strength charges, and load-based licensing of sewage treatment is being progressively introduced to give the operators of sewage treatment plants the opportunity to reduce the environmental impacts of their discharges.

In **Germany,** the principle of full cost-recovery applies to wastewater services as it does to water services. Charges in **Austria** also reflect the full costs of providing sewage services. In **Finland,** municipalities are strongly encouraged by law to collect user charges and connection charges to cover the full costs incurred by wastewater treatment activities.

In a number of countries, the proceeds of special pollution charges are channelled into a fund, which then redistributes specific subsidies or "soft-loans" for investing in wastewater treatment facilities. This occurs, for example, in **France** and in **Spain,** through the River Basin Agencies. A similar system existed in the **Netherlands** until 1997, but revenues from the charge are now used to finance research. However, industrial users which discharge into the public system in that country can still receive a discount per population equivalent of discharge. Since the public facility is designed to handle a certain capacity, the discount for large users (subsidy) is maintained, in order to prevent these users from developing their own treatment facilities, which would significantly increase the costs associated with the remaining population equivalent discharges.

8.5. Cross-subsidies

In a number of cases, water tariffs discriminate between different classes of users and cross-subsidies appear to be in place. Thus, although subsidies were abolished in 1994 in the **Czech Republic,** some cross-subsidies from industrial users to domestic users were maintained during a transitional period, to alleviate the impact of high water prices on households following the removal of subsidies.

Similarly, volumetric rates for industrial users in **Greece** are generally higher than for households. In **Italy,** an increasing-block tariff structure enables water companies to offer a subsidised tariff for the lower consumption block to domestic users. In **Japan,** charges are based on the relative payment capacity of each customer class, and there are cross-subsidies between customer classes. In **Korea,** domestic water users pay much less than industrial users, but this difference has recently been reduced, as a result of general price increases.

Water tariffs in many OECD countries are becoming more cost-reflective between different user groups. This has been partly driven by an increased desire to reflect marginal costs, and partly by the growing pressure from large industrial concerns that their charges reflect only the costs of assets and water which provide a service to them.

Cross-subsidies also exist between user classes for wastewater discharges and treatment. Thus, a cross-subsidisation for **Danish** agriculture exists, in the form of an annual payment of 65 million DKr under the Waterfund Law, to waterworks and borings that have been especially hard hit by pollution, mainly from pesticides (Wallach, 1996). These costs reflect the negative externalities of past intensive farming practices, which are now being covered by the general taxpayer.

127|

In the **US,** a 1996 survey of industrial pretreatment plants revealed that, in most cases, only limited information was available concerning the costs of providing services to specific classes of customer. As a result, multiple levels of cross-subsidisation existed within the pretreatment programmes, and between pretreatment and other municipal activities. Without providing exact figures, it was concluded that the cross-subsidies in place generally resulted in underpricing services to industrial users of wastewater services, which in turn led to under-investments in source reduction and pretreatment by these users (Koplow, Clark *et al.*, 1996).

Chapter 9

Effects of Water Pricing on Demand

In principle, water pricing can be used as a "demand management" tool, encouraging either a general reduction in the use of water and water services, or a specific reduction at certain peak times or seasons, through temporal variations in tariffs. In practice, there are concerns that the responsiveness of water demands to price levels and/or price structures (*i.e.* the "price elasticities") may be too low to induce water consumers to change their behaviour. There are a number of factors which may inhibit consumer responses to water pricing signals. These include:

- the price may be set so low that the economic "relevance" of the charge to the consumer is not very high. For example, a small charge to a person with a high income will not be a very significant element of the monthly budget;

- consumers require a certain minimum level of water just to exist. Up to that level, they will pay whatever they have to, in order to gain access to the water;

- the more complex a charging scheme is, the higher the proportion of consumers will be who are unlikely to be able to understand it fully, and therefore will be unable to react "rationally" to it;

- consumers may possess imperfect technical and financial information concerning the technologies available for economising on the use of water, or for reducing the volume (or the strength) of effluents that are generated; and

- most pricing systems for commercial enterprises are designed on the assumption that firms will attempt to maximise profits – but there may be alternative commercial objectives at work (especially in the short-term), such as revenue or sales maximisation.

Despite these limitations, available evidence suggests that price change *do* have some effects on demand, in certain circumstances and conditions. An overview of recent evidence related to this question is provided in the remainder of this chapter.

9.1. Effects of price changes on household water demand

As discussed in Chapter 5, household water prices have increased significantly in recent years in some OECD countries, notably **Denmark, France, Hungary,** the **Czech Republic,** and **Luxembourg.** A *priori*, the effects on water demand from this group seem clear, when compared with the data provided in Table 1. Five countries with substantial recent real increases in charges for various reasons (in three of them, subsidy reduction was the dominant cause) have each been characterised by falling household water consumption.

As seen above (Box 7), the water utility in Copenhagen (**Denmark**) has sought to have individual apartment household's water charges made clear to each household, even where these charges are determined non-volumetrically, in order to achieve the water conservation objective of reducing *per capita* domestic consumption from 134 lhd in 1995 to 110 lhd by the year 2000. This increased transparency in the value of the water services households utilise is necessary because water charges were previously included with a number of other services (even the monthly rent), thus "dulling" any pricing incentives for water conservation.

Correlations between increased water pricing and demand reduction are more heterogeneous for countries which have experienced more moderate water tariff increases. In **England and Wales,** for example, there has been full cost recovery on all direct economic costs for many years now, but the low metering penetration of households (and thus, the frequent absence of any volumetric price signals at all) means that underlying domestic consumption continues to increase.

Table 23 summarises some recent evidence on metering effects in single-family houses in OECD countries. These studies, like those listed in the earlier report (OECD, 1987a; Table 16), continue to show significant demand reduction effects resulting from domestic metering. It is noteworthy that the size of the effects on *peak* demands are often much greater than those on *average* demands. This indicates that temporal variations in prices are likely to be particularly effective in smoothing out demand peaks.

Table 24 lists the results of the few available studies which have reported the demand effects of introducing volumetric charges for individual apartments. Again, these indicate that the introduction of metering for water consumption can have a significant effect on reducing consumption levels.

Tables 25 and 26 present recent evidence on the effects on household demands of changes in tariff *structures* and tariff *prices*, respectively. The results are unsurprising. The tariff structure effects all have the anticipated sign, although the more recent price elasticity estimates continue to show generally lower values for Europe than for other countries.[20]

When interpreting Table 26, it is useful to note that consumers will sometimes react to price signals even if they are not directly affected by increased prices. For

Table 23. **Estimated Water Savings Due to Metering and Charging by Volume**

Primarily in Single-Family Houses

CS/TS	Location	Period	Comparison	Savings due to metering	Reference
TS	Collingwood, Ontario, Canada	1986-90		Summer peak: 37%	Anon (1992)
TS	Leavenworth, Washington, US	1988-91		Summer peak: 61%	Anon(1993)
CS	9 metering trial sites, England	1988-92	7 000 houses in 9 trial groups and 9 control groups	Average figure: 11.9%	Herrington (1997a)
TS	Isle of Wight, England	1988-92	Metered population rose from 1% to 97% in 1992 (50 000 homes)	Annual: 21.3%	DOE (1993)
CS	Metering trial sites, England	1988-92	Peak hr/day/wk/month: – hot, dry summers – wet summers:	39%/27%/35%/27% 4%/15%/19%/15%	Herrington (1997a)
TS + CS	Mataro, Spain	1983-93	25 694 hh's in 1983 (M: 29%) with 39 952 hh's in 1993 (M: 90%)	Annual: 35%*	Sanclemente (undated)
CS	Terrassa, Spain	1994-95	23 400 UM hh's and 34 038 M hh's	Annual: 12.7%	Sanclemente (undated)
TS	Barcelona, Spain	early 1990s	2 927 connections switched UM to M	Annual: 12.8%	Sanclemente (undated)
TS	East Anglia, UK	1990s		Annual: 15-20% Summer peak: 25-35%	Edwards (1996)
TS	Portland, US	1993-94		Annual: 10-12%	Dietz and Ranton (1995)
TS	New York City, US	1991-95		Annual: 7.4%	Environment Agency (1996)
TS	Oaks Park, Kent, UK	1993-96	61 houses	Annual: 27.5% Summer peak: up to 50%	Mid-Kent (1997)
TS	St. Peters, Kent, UK	1993-96	160 houses	Annual: 14.1% Summer peak: up to 32%	Mid-Kent (1997)

Notes:
CS   Cross-sectional study.
TS   Time-series study.
M   Metered.
UM   Unmetered.
*   Income effect of +10% in 10 years assumed.

OECD 1999

Table 24. **Impacts of Metering Individual Apartments**

All Time-series Studies

Location	Years	Average consumption		Saving	Reference
		Before metering	After metering		
Nancy, France: 120-apartment building	1980-82	220 m³/yr.	120 m³/yr.	45%	Roseberg (1994)
Paris, France: 200-apartment building	1986-87	160 m³/yr.	120 m³/yr.	25%	Roseberg (1994)
Rennes, France: 32-apartment building	1987-89	115 m³/yr.	83 m³/yr.	28%	Roseberg (1994)
Copenhagen, Denmark: apartment building	Early 1990s			30-35%	Sanclemente (undated)
Hamburg, Germany				15%	Kraemer and Nowell-Smith* (1997)

* Quoting Hamburger Wasserwerke, 28.

example, **German** experience suggests that households in apartment blocks will reduce their demand, even if they share a meter with several other households. In this situation, it is improved general information (rather than a direct price signal) that is driving the reduction in demand.

However, even with the evidence presented here, a number of uncertainties remain regarding the effects on household demand of changes in water pricing structures and levels. As with most demand functions, it is often only after a certain threshold change in price levels that consumption levels will respond elastically. In addition, increasing prices (and increasing revenues) can sometimes be associated with better infrastructure or improved water quality. Where this is the case, the higher quality of water and of service provided may actually lead to *increased* consumption, despite the higher price levels. Substitution effects – in terms of self-supply – also need to be considered, and particularly the resulting effects on peak demand.

Box 14 and Table 27 also provide an indication of the responsiveness of water demands in the **UK** to "peak-pricing" practices – in this case, to "seasonal" and "time-of-day" tariffs.

Substantial recent price increases in the **Czech Republic** have evidently been associated with substantial decreases in the consumption of drinking water, indicating a relatively high price elasticity of demand, and this trend is expected to continue in the future (Pavlík, 1996: 3, 5).

The conclusion that demand does not vary significantly when prices are changed is at least somewhat countered by the empirical observation that metering still causes considerable political debate when it is proposed. Arguments about the

Table 25. **Consumption Effects from Tariff *Structure* Changes**

Location	Year(s)	Tariff before	Tariff after	Consumption before (lhd)	Saving	Reference
United Water Co., NY, US	1981	IB, non-seasonal	Seasonal rate 150% higher		Aver: 20% Peak ratio down from 1.75 to 1.5[1]	Environment Agency (1996)
Palm Beach, US	1983-8	IB and then DB	IB	Aver: 760; Large users > 2 500	14% in large user category[2]	Federico (1990)
Barcelona, Spain	1989-96	2 × IB	3 × IB, with much higher price for 3rd block	211 (1991)	c. 10%[3]	Sanclemente (cited in Harrington, 1998)
San Antonio, Texas, US	1994-6	3 × IB + 10% seasonal surcharge	4 × IB + seasonal surcharge	Winter: 252 Summer: 469	Total: 12% to 14%[4] Summer: 22%	Fox (1995)

Notes:
IB   Increasing-block.
DB   Decreasing-block.
1.   Consumption then continued rising at about 1.6% per year.
2.   A "pure" price effect.
3.   A tariff change occurred in 1989. No consumption estimate was available for 1988 or 1989; the nearest estimate is for 1991. The 1996 estimate was 193 lhd.
4.   Revenue-neutral, with small conservation fund raised.

Table 26. *Price* **Elasticities for Public Water Supply**

Location	Type of model	Year(s)	Elasticities	Reference
Australia				
Sydney Water	TS/OLS	1959-60 to 1993-4	AR: −0.13	Warner (1995)
Denmark				
Copenhagen	TS/OLS		−0.10	Hansen (1996)
France				
116 eastern communes	CS-TS/Panel	1988-93	AP, s/r: −0.22 AP, l/r: −0.26 MP, s/r: −0.18	Nauges and Thomas (1998)
Gironde	CS/OLS		−0.17	Point (1993)
Italy				
Unknown	CS	Mid-1990s	−0.24	Critelli (1998)
Korea	TS	1998	−0.29	Kim (1998)
New Zealand				
Auckland	TS		−0.08	Law (1986)
Auckland	CS	1976	−0.20	Law (1986)
Auckland	CS	1981	−0.24	Law (1986)
Christchurch	CS/CBS	Late 1980s	−0.29	Welsh (1991)
Sweden				
282 of 286 Swedish communities	CS-TS/Panel	1980-92	AP, l/r: −0.20 MP, l/r: −0.10	Höglund (1997)
US				
Wisconsin	CS/OLS		−0.12	Schafter and David (1985)
Illinois	CS/SEs		−0.71	Chicoine et al. (1986)
Illinois	CS-TS OLS		−0.48	Chicoine and Ramamurthy (1986)
Denton, Texas	CS-TS IV,2SLS		IBR: −0.86 DBR: −0.36	Nieswiadomy and Molina (1989)
Massachusetts	CS		−0.40/−0.45	Stevens, Millan and Willis (1992)
Santa Barbara, California	CS-TS/2SLS		−0.33	Renwick and Archibald (1997)

Notes:

TS	Times series	l/r	Long-run
OLS	Ordinary least squares	s/r	Short-run
CS	Cross-sectional	AR	Average revenue
Panel	Panel data techniques	AP	Average price
CBS	Contingent behaviour survey	MP	Marginal price
SEs	Simultaneous equations	IBR	Increasing-block rate
IV	Instrumental variable	DBR	Decreasing-block rate
2SLS	Two-stage least squares		

behavioural impact of domestic metering are still helping to shape water policy in at least three OECD countries (**Ireland, New Zealand,** and the **UK**), and a new area of public debate has developed in recent years concerning the metering of individual apartments (see Chapter 5).

Box 14.   Price Effects on Time-of-day and Seasonal Demands in England

In the **UK,** small-scale site metering trials were conducted in 1988-92 which introduced time-of-day tariffs in two areas. In the Lee Valley Water Company (Brookmans Park trial), a complex time-of-day tariff for water supply was designed with two diurnal peak rates, and augmented by a seasonal factor. However, the tariff was abandoned after being used for one year, in favour of a constant volumetric rate.

The second trial, by Wessex Water Company (Broadstone), compared 358 "affluent suburban properties" in the trial group, with 625 similar houses in the control group. Here, the trial was sustained for all three charging years (1989-90 to 1991-92), and the peak rate was defined for a three-hour period each evening consistently throughout the year, with the price at this time being 77 per cent higher than for the rest of the day. This trial was also for water supply only, with sewerage and sewage treatment again being charged according to a single volumetric rate, with no temporal variation.

Peak-hour and peak-day demands were found to be significantly affected by metering in the first two years of charging, with peak hour demands falling in "trial" households by an average of 17 per cent, and peak day demands by 23 per cent, as compared with what would have been expected in an unmetered situation (calculated by comparison with what happened in "control" households). However, there are some qualifications to these results: *i*) these percentages may have been influenced by very cold weather (and therefore by "bursts", generating peak demands over which households had no control); *ii*) the apparent peak day effect is no greater than that reported (on average) for all the trial areas, including nine without any time-of-day tariffs; and *iii*) in the third year of charging in Broadstone, daily and hourly peaks actually *rose* more in the trial than in the control area (Water Research Centre, 1994).

Reliable data is also available from two trials with seasonal charging variations over a three-year period. These were based in the Southern Water Company (at Chandler's Ford, where 602 trial homes were compared with 280 control properties), and in East Worcestershire Water (1 100 trial and 600 control houses). In both cases, a small annual fixed charge was imposed, together with: *i*) (in winter) a low volumetric rate applying to all consumption; and *ii*) (in summer) the same low rate applying to the base load (defined as being equal to the previous winter's consumption) plus a summer premium rate applied to all consumption in excess of the base load. In both trials, the summer premium tariff was fixed at just over 60 per cent more than the base tariff.

In Table 27, the estimated average effects of domestic metering on summer and winter demands are separately distinguished for both the two trials of seasonal tariffs described above, and the other seven of the nine trials in England and Wales for which a summer/winter distinction could be made. It can be seen that the impact of metering in summer is significantly more marked in those trials which included summer premium rates (Water Research Centre, 1994).

Source: DOE (1993).

135

Table 27. **Estimated Average Metering Effects by Season in UK Metering Trials**

Per cent

	6 summer months	6 winter months
Two seasonal tariff trials	−21.1	−7.5
Seven non-seasonal tariff trials	−10.5	−6.4
All nine trials areas	−12.9	−6.6

9.2. Effects of price changes on industrial water demand

Because of the specificity of consumption in the industrial sector, it is difficult to obtain reliable data summarising the price elasticity of industrial water demands. However, there are some indications that industrial water users may be more responsive in their water-demand behaviour to price changes than other water users, particularly households. This is both because industrial users tend to have a greater commitment to finding and exploiting cost-savings, and because they often have a greater range of available water-conserving technologies to draw upon.

9.3. Effects of price changes on agricultural water demand

Estimating agricultural water demand elasticities has attracted much attention, as arid and semi-arid industrialised countries have experienced increasing periods of water scarcity. In general, most available estimates seem to indicate some degree of demand elasticity. In other words, farmers *do* seem to react moderately to water price levels, to water application costs, and to water shortages. However, there is also substantial evidence that water rates and irrigation technologies can be more intensively influenced by other factors (such as climate variations, agricultural policies, product prices, or structural factors), than they are by prices.

Among the many studies characterising water demand functions in the agricultural sector, several conclusions stand out as being of particular empirical interest:

– Water demand is usually inelastic only up to a given price level. This "price threshold" depends on: *i*) the economic productivity of the water; *ii*) the set of alternative production strategies that farmers actually adopt in order to substitute for water consumption; *iii*) proportion of land devoted to permanently-irrigated crops; *iv*) the irrigation technologies in place; and *v*) the size of the water allotment. Table 28 provides selected research results concerning irrigation demand elasticities, as evaluated in different contexts.

– The "price threshold" indicates possibilities for increasing water charges without significantly perturbing farming activities. Although net farm returns would be reduced by price increases, these (operating) losses would eventually be captured by reductions in the (capital) values of land.

Table 28. **Cross-sectional Price Elasticity Estimates for Irrigation Demands**

Source	Method/context	Region/country	Water demand elasticity
Moore *et al.* (1994)	Groundwater price variations	US Northwest	−11.72
	Econometric model	US Central plains	3.99
	Cross-sectional data	US Southwest	−16.88
		US Southern plains	−2.16
Garrido *et al.* (1998)	Institutional price simulations	Spain (Andalusia)	LP: −0.06; MP: −1.00
	Dynamic math programming	Spain (Andalusia)	LP: −0.12; MP: −0.48
	model	Spain (Castile)	LP: −0.09; MP: −0.26
	Long-term results	Spain (Castile)	LP: −0.00; MP: −0.03
Montginoul and Rieu (1996)	Math programming models over 170 irrigated farms	France (La Charente)	LP: −0.04; MP: −0.27

Notes:
LP = Low water price ranges.
MP = Medium water price ranges.

- Farmer responses to price increases could include: *i*) changes in cropping patterns; *ii*) reductions in the amount of irrigated land; *iii*) improvements in on-farm water management practices; *iv*) changes in irrigation technologies; and *v*) abandonment of irrigation altogether.

- Price increases, combined with more efficient distribution systems, might actually end up increasing total water consumption. This could result from the net reduction of on-farm water costs caused by the reduction of leakages in the water distribution system. The volume of water returns generated in the irrigation district as a whole might then be reduced more than the reduction in the amount of water demanded on the farm. As a result, the basin's water balance might actually be *worsened* by price increases.

- The adoption of more efficient irrigation technologies is accelerated by higher water charges, or higher water application costs. But other factors, such as land quality, well depths, and agricultural output prices are just as important, if not more so, than the price effect of water itself.

- Subsidies to the rehabilitation of irrigation districts, and to new irrigation technologies might end up increasing on-farm water consumption. Although water productivity, measured as revenues per cubic meter used, would increase, total water consumption at the level of the basin might also increase, unless allotments are simultaneously revised downwards.

- Cross-sectional studies of irrigation districts, both at the national and international levels, have found conflicting evidence of the influence of water price levels on water management efficiencies.

Chapter 10
Social Tariffs and Affordability

10.1. Access to public water supply

Accessibility figures for basic water utility services, such as piped water or domestic sewage would normally be expected to be at (or very near) economic limits for most OECD countries, and thereby to change very little over time. Access levels should also be less than 100 per cent in most countries, reflecting the presumed inefficiency of linking rural households to existing networks. Thus, only **Denmark, Finland,** and **Sweden** among the "mature" OECD Europe water economies exhibit public water supply access figures of 90 per cent or less, and all have sizeable rural populations (Figure 6). The four EU Cohesion Fund countries, however, indicate generally lower access rates, ranging from 80 per cent in **Ireland,** to over 90 per cent in **Spain.**

Access rates to public sewage systems are much more variable. As a result, sewage access often seems to bear surprisingly little relation to PWS access (*e.g.* **Hungary, Japan, Portugal, Poland, Spain,** and **Turkey**). All four EU Cohesion Fund countries indicate sewage access for 55-70 per cent of their populations – figures similar to those for **Mexico** and **Turkey.** Assuming that "economic limits" have not yet been reached in these countries, significant economic investment seems to be implied for them in the future, since the 30-45 per cent of the population remaining to be connected will, of course, be the most costly to add to the system.

Overall, therefore, domestic access to public water supply and sewage treatment facilities is quite high in the majority of OECD Member countries. Although there is still room for improvement, the social and public health requirements for universal access to domestic water supply are already largely being fulfilled.

Another dimension of access is affordability. In this context, however, water services providers are increasingly realising the inefficiencies (both economic and environmental) associated with offering "across-the-board" low water prices to domestic consumers in order to ensure that affordable water is available for those in need. Instead of this type of "blanket" subsidy, the increasing tendency is to either support general income levels directly (for example, through direct payments, rather

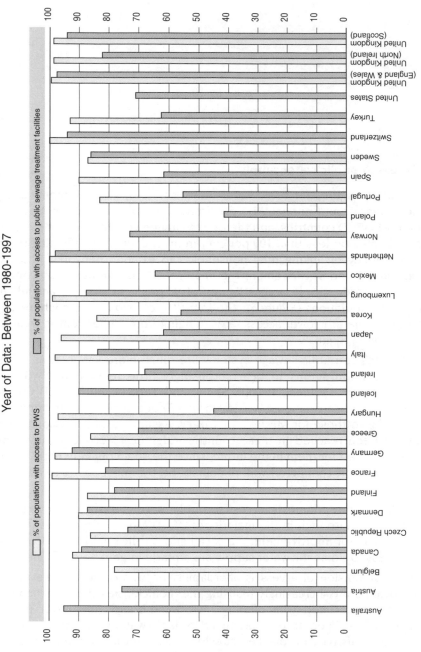

Figure 6. Access to Public Water Supply and Sewage Treatment Facilities in Selected OECD Countries
Year of Data: Between 1980-1997

☐ % of population with access to PWS

▦ % of population with access to public sewage treatment facilities

Source: OECD (1999c).

than via alterations to water tariff or pricing structures), or to better target tariff reforms to ensure that reduced water prices reach those most in need. As seen earlier, a number of countries use tariff structures – such as increasing-block tariffs or free initial allowances – that ensure that consumers of all income levels have access to the minimum requirements for water services at affordable prices.

In the remainder of this chapter, both the "micro" and "macro" aspects of the affordability of household water services are examined, with the notion of "affordability" referring to the extent to which households can afford the water services that they choose (or are obliged) to purchase. The "micro" issue concentrates on affordability for the less well-off. The ways in which governments and water utilities have chosen to address this issue can be divided into two broad groups, emphasising either the tariffs themselves (tariff-based solutions) or certain types of households (target group solutions). Tariff solutions can be found either in tariff specification, tariff amendment, or tariff innovation. Target group solutions focus on assistance to either individual households or specified groups of households. This assistance may be provided using two basic forms of tariff innovation: via tariff discounts (lower prices) or via income support (higher incomes).

For both types of solution, funding may ultimately originate from outside government bodies, although the tariff-based approach is more likely in practice to be self-financed within the utility (*i.e.* through some form of cross-subsidisation). Such cross-subsidisation can, and does, occur both from non-household sectors (*e.g.* industry) to the household sector, or between different groups within the household sector itself (*i.e.* from high-income to low-income customers). Similarly, in target group solutions, price reductions can be funded by the government (although in practice, they normally involve cross-subsidisation between water consumers), and income transfers can originate from the utility itself (although social security is the more usual source).

The two approaches of tariff-based and target group solutions are not mutually exclusive. A new tariff can be partly reserved for certain groups of consumers (*e.g.* those in receipt of social security benefits), or it can be partly geared to some indicator of low income, such as property value or property type.

A focus on the "macro" aspects of affordability is also provided below, via a brief examination of two possible indicators of the overall affordability of water services for households within a country. Effectively, this means comparing the average (or typical) water bill in a country with an average household's financial strength, or "ability to pay".

10.2. Tariff-based solutions to affordability problems

Tariff specification solutions

"Tariff specification" refers to the use of increasing-block tariffs for achieving social objectives. **Italy, Greece, Spain, Portugal** and **Belgium** all apply increasing-block schedules, based on the claim that these are advantageous to the relatively poor, and each country grants low-income consumers the opportunity to buy "early" blocks of water at low prices. It is not known whether a similar line of argument is responsible for the popularity of such tariffs in many Asian countries (including **Korea** and **Japan**), or its occasional incidence in the **Netherlands** and **Australia.**

However, increasing-block schedules do not necessarily reflect large equity gains for the poor. A relatively small "first block" range may simply mean that nearly all households of average size or above are "forced" into higher (and more expensive) blocks, so the consequent welfare distribution may be small, as compared with a uniform volumetric rate.[21] Large poor families may therefore end up in much more expensive blocks, and could pay significantly higher average volumetric rates, than smaller (but higher-income) households under an increasing-block structure.

Nevertheless, there is an underlying social appeal to such tariff structures, and recognising the significance of one- and two-pensioner households among the emerging poor in a number of developed economies, there is a sizeable reservoir of income redistribution opportunities available to governments by using increasing-block tariff systems, so long as the widths and prices of these blocks are carefully chosen.

One general *caveat* is in order, however. This occurs when a minimum charge is levied which covers a relatively large block of "initial" consumption. Thus, in **Japan,** it has been common for utilities to specify a minimum charge covering 10 m^3 per month since at least the 1960s, when domestic consumption was significantly lower than it is today. The same situation exists in **Korea.** In Taegu City, for example, the 1974 minimum charge "paid for" the first 15 m^3/month, even though estimated consumption was only 62 lhd, such that only households with nine or more people were likely to be facing a non-zero price for water. In 1997, just before the abandonment of the "basic rate", only a three-person household (or larger) in Taegu would normally have expected to face a positive price.

In general, it would be better to eliminate the minimum charge, thereby removing its potential to dampen the conservation "message", and to replace it with a more carefully-sculpted fixed customer charge, aimed specifically at residential households.

Tariff amendment solutions

Amending tariffs is best seen as an attempt to make increasing-block structures more "friendly" to households with below-average incomes, but of average (or above-average) size. It may be pursued by relating either the fixed charge element or one or more characteristics of the cheap blocks (size, price) to the "needs" of households. Three examples of current practice may be offered:

- In the Flanders region of **Belgium,** as discussed earlier, the first 15 m^3 per annum *per person* (equivalent to 41 lhd) in each household has been provided free since 1 January 1997. This has the virtue of being: *i*) small enough to ensure that very few households will face a zero price for their water; *ii*) "politically defensible" by covering a certain core of basic (essential) water use in the home; and *iii*) "equitable", especially between households of different sizes. However, as discussed above, this may lead to some unexpected effects on both water prices (for those units consumed which are paid for) and water demand. This system is believed to be the only operational example of such a tariff anywhere in the world, although a similar schedule has also been proposed for **England and Wales** (Herrington, 1996).

- In **Spain,** two innovations for Barcelona have already been noted: a "blunter" version of the Flanders size-of-household amendment (this time, extending the width of the second block, in line with any household size in excess of five persons), and a progressive variation in the fixed charge, depending on the type of property occupied by the household. Similarly, Madrid and Seville are understood to have introduced new or amended social tariffs in recent years.

- The third example comes from the **US,** where the Los Angeles Mayor's Blue Ribbon Committee on Water Rates created a radically different rate schedule between 1992 and 1994 (Box 15). This abolished the old minimum charge; introduced summer premia (to increase volumetric prices up to long-run marginal cost levels); and created a two-tier rate structure, in which the size of the first tier is in line with important determinants of what a "responsible" household would be expected to consume. In this way, economic efficiency, equity, and environmental concerns are all addressed.

France is also in the development stages of such tariff structures, with a social tariff for domestic water use currently under study, and the possibility of a forthcoming modification to Article 13 of the Water Law of 3 January 1992 to allow the introduction of a reduced tariff for small consumers.

Tariff innovation solutions

In some circumstances, no tariff amendment will be able to capture the degree of change required. In this case, completely new tariffs may be required. Examples are available from two very different types of water utilities: one from Anglian Water in the **UK** (population served: 4 million) and one involving a group of initiatives from the over 100 communes supplying water services in **Luxembourg** (average population served: 3 500) (Eurostat, 1997).

In recent years, Anglian Water in the **UK** has chosen to introduce completely new tariffs to meet the concerns of those who object (on social equity grounds) to any sudden shift from flat-fee charges (based essentially on property values) to metering (and the associated volumetric charging that goes with it), which is not accompanied by complete freedom of choice in tariff selection. Opponents were

143

Box 15.   Los Angeles Tariff Reform in the Early 1990s

The Mayor's Blue Ribbon Committee on Water Rates (1992) initially reported the results of an inquiry into the pre-1992 rate structure. It found serious drawbacks to the "old" system operated by the Los Angeles Department of Water and Power (serving nearly four million people), whose mandate had been to develop a water rate structure that was "equitable and promotes conservation, water recycling, and improved water quality".

The main drawbacks were identified as: i) the "old" structure failed to inform customers of future rising costs; ii) water shortages, and hence appeals to conserve, were inevitably associated with rate increases (due to the size of short-run fixed costs); iii) assistance was unreasonably restricted to single-family homes (SFHs), whereas needy groups were increasingly locating in multi-family residences (MFRs); iv) the existence of a fixed minimum monthly charge encouraged wastage; and v) in order to receive the full benefits of water at discounted prices, low-income consumers had to consume more than a certain quantity, which again led to wastage.

To remove these disadvantages, the Mayor's Committee, following extensive public hearings in 1994, proposed:

- the abolition of the minimum charge;
- the payment to low-income customers of credits in cash terms (and independent of water usage); and
- relating the size of the first tier of water use (at base price) for SFH users to household "needs".

These needs were to be determined by lot-size (five categories), temperature zone (three in all), and family size (there would be an extra first-tier allowance for each resident in the household in excess of six). Additionally, an inexplicably small summer premium for all users of first tier water was introduced, ranging between 2-4 per cent.

All additional (or second-tier) water for SFH users would be priced at higher levels: at a price 37 per cent higher than the first-tier in the winter, and at a price 72 per cent higher in the summer (June to October). For MFR consumers, all winter water was priced at first tier-rates (very similar to those for SFHs), but in summer, first-tier usage was fixed at 125 per cent of the average consumption of the preceding winter. Any consumption after that would have a price that was 72 per cent higher. The summer second-tier rate for both SFHs and MFRs was set to reflect the forward-looking unit costs of Los Angeles having to add new supplies (i.e. marginal costs). All these rates and arrangements became effective on 1 June 1995.

---

particularly concerned about compulsory metering programmes which Anglian proposed in "resource-stretched" areas. Anglian's reactions to a determined opposition campaign were first to abandon all compulsory programmes other than those centred on new homes or on the use of certain high-water-use luxury appliances, and then to introduce a new tariff (the SoLow rate), which has no standing charge, but which includes a volumetric rate some 25 per cent higher than that contained in the "normal" tariff. As Table 29 illustrates, a very low-water-using household (a single person, using 100 lhd) which uses both the Anglian water supply and sewerage services would, in 1998-99, save about £20 a year by electing to go onto the SoLow tariff.

Table 29. **Household Metered Charges in Anglian Water (1998-99)**

Litres per *household* per day (lhhd)

		Normal tariff	SoLow tariff	Plus 4 tariff*
Standing Charge	(£/year)	36.00	–	137.00
Volumetric rate	(£/m³)	2.12	2.62	1.04
Annual bill:	36.5 m³/yr. (100 lhhd)	113.39	95.56	175.13
	50 m³/yr. (137 lhhd)	142.01	130.90	189.23
	100 m³/yr. (274 lhhd)	248.02	261.80	241.47
	150 m³/yr. (411 lhhd)	354.03	392.70	293.70
	200 m³/yr. (548 lhhd)	460.04	523.60	345.94

*   Consumers receiving social security benefits (Income Support, Job Seekers Allowance or Family Credit) may choose *any* of the three tariffs. All other consumers may choose between Normal and SoLow;

Although this innovative tariff would benefit all households using less than 72 m³ per annum, the SoLow rate is of no help to households of average- or above-average size, especially those unemployed or in low-paid work. Anglian has therefore introduced another specific rate for these groups for 1998-99: the "Plus 4" rate which combines a high standing charge with a low volumetric rate. Table 29 also illustrates that annual savings associated with Plus 4, relative to normal tariffs, rise from about £5 to about £115, as consumption increases from 100 to 200 m³ per annum.

These new tariffs serve two main purposes. First, in a general sense, they demonstrate that water utilities can be responsive to different social contexts. Second, by "carving out" new tariff structures, they can give real benefits to otherwise disadvantaged consumers.

In **Luxembourg,** there are examples of communes charging households increasing-block tariffs, but gearing the widths of these blocks to the number of people in the household. Table 30 shows one such example.

In another commune, the water tariff is gradually reduced, according to the increase in the number of children in the household (Table 31).

145

Table 30. **Variation in Block-size: Luxembourg Commune (1996-97)**

Water price in Flux/m³	Consumption in m³ per year in households consisting of:						
	1 person	2 persons	3 persons	4 persons	5 persons	6 persons	7 persons
40	≤ 60	≤ 100	≤ 140	≤ 180	≤ 220	≤ 260	≤ 300
50	61-70	101-120	141-170	181-220	221-270	261-320	301-370
70	> 71	> 121	> 171	> 221	> 271	> 321	> 371

Table 31. **Volumetric Rate, Depending on the Number of Children: Luxembourg Commune (1996-97)**

Standard household tariff	38.0 Flux/m³
Family with 3 children	26.6 Flux/m³
Family with 4 children	22.8 Flux/m³
Family with 5 or more children	19.0 Flux/m³

These "socially-driven" variations inspire significant differences in basic tariff structures, with 118 communes in Luxembourg currently charging for water at 118 different prices. There are increasing-block, decreasing-block, and constant volumetric rate schedules for water supply; while for sewerage and sewage treatment, equally exotic arrangements are to be found, combining one or more elements from fixed charges (per household, per person or per person-equivalent) and charges per m³ supplied (with or without different maxima and minima, or only coming into operation with supplies over a certain limit).

What these examples show is that it is quite possible to design tariffs – with entry being either restricted or unrestricted – which protect the interests of well-defined groups, be they low-income households, large households, households with children, etc. In each case, there will normally be a trade-off arising from the innovation. But what is lost in efficiency, to be set against the gains in equity, depends very much on the starting-point for the comparison.

Using the Anglian Water example, if the initial case is considered to be an unmetered consumer (*i.e.* one subject to some sort of flat-fee system), the gains from the transition in terms of a positive marginal price – leading to improved economic and environmental signals – have to be set against not only the extra costs of establishing and operating a volumetric charging system, but also against any hardship which may result from the more complex matrix of gains and losses for individual households. Implicitly, the tariff innovators must believe that the extra gains in equity from the introduction of the two "new" tariffs outweigh the more subtle efficiency losses, which may occur because the volumetric rate is not exactly "right" (*i.e.* perhaps drifting further away from a marginal cost base, such as is presumably true of the very low price attached to the Plus 4 tariff).

Support for this "implicit" view is provided by the relatively low price elasticities for household use (Chapter 7), and the further argument that the beneficiaries of the restricted Plus 4 tariff are unlikely, by definition, to have significant luxury uses of water. In **Luxembourg** as well, the issue of whether the going price is 40, 50 or 70 Flux (Table 30), or anything from 19-38 Flux (Table 31) is probably considered to be of secondary importance, when considered alongside the potential equity gains to be achieved.

Tariff choice solutions

In some circumstances, the gains from tariff innovation may result not so much from the introduction of a new tariff, as from the fact of offering consumers a new choice. In terms of consumer welfare, adding a new tariff and allowing genuine freedom of choice will always lead to some consumers being better off, without others being worse off, so long as the numbers of consumers electing to "join" any of the tariffs has no feedback effects on the specific characteristics of the other tariffs (*e.g.* on their volumetric rates). It is precisely the importance of that qualification that has led Anglian Water to restrict entry to its Plus 4 tariff. If it had not done so, all high users of water would – rationally – have sought to subscribe to Plus 4, and the company would have then needed to replace its lost revenue from tariff changes elsewhere. It is clear that important issues of public relations and price discrimination are therefore also bound up with this question.

Two types of choice can be found in OECD countries. First, there is the flat-fee/metering choice by consumers, which is clearly appropriate where the demand-supply balance in a particular location is such that a case for universal metering cannot yet be established. Such a choice exists in **England and Wales, Scotland,** and in Antwerp (**Belgium**). It would also generally enhance equity in other largely "flat-fee countries" (**Norway** and **New Zealand,** for example), since the initial capital costs can (and should) in those situations be at the metering optant's expense, with the extra reading, billing, and collection costs normally being reflected in the fixed charges paid by households.

The other type of choice is the one provided by Anglian Water (**UK**) in its desire to see metering become much more widespread. In public relation terms, this choice has been presented essentially as a measure to "smooth out" the transition process. A separate question then emerges. Looking ahead, if Anglian arrives – say, in ten years time – at a more-or-less fully-metered situation, would it then be desirable to maintain the option choice(s) originally on offer? The case for some assistance with water bills for lower income groups will presumably still be strong. Indeed, given recent trends in charges and increasing recognition and recovery of environmental costs, the case may be even stronger.

147

Presumably, a single charging structure that attempted to be fair to all consumers would then be the ideal, and here, the recent initiatives in **Flanders**, **Barcelona**, and **Los Angeles** are relevant. All these innovations have in common the fact that they represent attempts to improve upon the equity attributes of increasing-block tariffs. Each also incorporates changes in either the sizes (widths) of one or other of the initial blocks in the structure, or in the fixed charge, according to perceived household needs. They are therefore important "models" for steady-state, fully metered, residential scenarios.

10.3. Target group solutions to affordability problems

Examples exist in OECD countries of both price (rate) reductions and income supplements (or "cashback") schemes aimed at assisting low-income households. For example, Sydney Water (**Australia**) reports a wide range of "residential safety nets", aimed at helping consumers who are experiencing financial difficulties in the transition to consumption-based charging. The main components of this system are:

- a Pensioner Rebate scheme, funded by the New South Wales government, which also decides the eligibility criteria for concession. Under this scheme, pensioners are given a 50 per cent discount on the availability (fixed) charge on their property, with no discount on water usage;
- a Payments Assistance scheme whereby customers experiencing genuine hardship may apply for a rebate on their current water bills; and
- a Kidney Dialysis Program, whereby full water allowances are granted to customers requiring the use of Continuous Flow Home Dialysis (400kl/year), Continuous Ambulatory Peritoneal Dialysis (12kl/year) or Recycled Water Dialysis (12kl/year).

A ceiling of A\$ 2 million per year (about 0.2 per cent of Sydney Water's total income) exists for hardship relief. In other Australian utilities in the past, rebates of up to 50 per cent on all water and wastewater charges had been granted to holders of a variety of concession cards (Herrington, 1997a).

There are also numerous examples in the **US** of disabled and low-income households receiving a wide variety of assistance, including rebates based on income, percentage discounts on water bills for certain groups, waivers of the fixed charge, and fixed allowances (or credits) on each bill. Most of this assistance is funded by individual utilities, although occasionally local authorities and voluntary community organisations (using donated funds) are also involved.

In 1997, however, the latest survey of US water rate characteristics found only 4 per cent of surveyed utilities offering discounts for low-volume consumers, and 9 per cent offering discounts for low-income consumers (Raftelis Environmental Consulting Group, 1998). 28 per cent of utilities offered "other" (unspecified) forms of assistance.

Beecher, writing in a US context (Beecher, 1994), claims that there are actually many more options available for utilities to offer assistance than is generally realised. These include financial counselling, forgiveness of arrears, payment discounts, income-based payments, lifeline rates, targeted conservation, disconnection moratoria, and flow restrictions.

At the same time, it should be noted that several western European countries suggested, in submissions to this report, that there were *no* significant affordability problems existing in those countries. This was the impression conveyed, for example, by information provided by the **Netherlands, Norway,** and **Sweden.** In Eastern Europe, however, the reverse is true, for example in **Hungary,** where some subsidies from the central government budget are "earmarked" for those utilities with the highest-cost local water and wastewater supplies.

10.4. Measures of aggregate affordability

In the absence of detailed information about the distribution of household water charges "aggregate affordability" involves relating some measure of average charges to either average household incomes, or (failing that) to average household aggregate expenditures.

Two attempts have been made here to devise relevant time series across OECD countries. First, the results of the latest (1996) IWSA household water bill survey (IWSA, 1997) have been built upon. Since 1992, this survey has been conducted every two years to establish the average public water supply bill (measured in ECU) of a standard four person household[22] in a number of cities in each of the participating IWSA members. The results, which exclude VAT and other consumption/sales taxes, may then be related to an indicator of purchasing power in each country.[23] The only such indicator easily available for a broad range of countries is the one used by IWSA itself: GDP *per capita* (in 1996 ECU). Column 1 of Table 32 therefore divides the average bill (for a household of four) in each country by the GDP *per capita* for the same year, in order to generate a rough indicator of average family public water supply expenditures, in relation to "average ability-to-pay".[24]

Because of the crudeness of GDP *per capita* as a surrogate for "ability-to-pay" (and also because of the scaling factor of 100), the absolute magnitude of the resulting series is irrelevant. However, the series is still of some interest, since it provides a rough indicator of relative average affordability across the OECD. Table 32 ranks countries according to the calculated (Column 1) statistics, with a fairly clear-cut division of the countries with available data into five groups. High values of the indicator reflect higher PWS charges relative to GDP *per capita*, and therefore relatively low average affordability (especially **Hungary,** the **Czech Republic,** and **Portugal**). At the other end of the spectrum, low figures imply high average affordability (**Italy, Norway, Korea,** the **US,** and **Iceland**).

149

Table 32.   **Measures of Overall (Average) Affordability of Water Charges**

	PWS charges for an average family of four, relative to GDP, and bsed on IWSA data (1996)	Average water charges as proportion of household incomes (Y) or expenditures (E) (1997/98)	Water charges as proportion of household incomes
Hungary	3.62	> 3%[1] (Y)	
Portugal	2.25		0.5%
Czech Republic	2.17		
Germany	1.32[2]		1.0%
Luxembourg	1.30	1.0-1.5% (Y)	
Netherlands	1.13	1.6%	
Austria	1.13	1.0-1.3% (Y)	
France	1.12		1.1%
Belgium	1.09		
England and Wales	1.05	1.3%[3] (Y)	1.2%
Canada	1.05		
Spain	1.02	1.0%[4] (Y)	0.4%
Finland	0.97		
Switzerland	0.94		
Turkey	(0.87)[5]	1.2-1.7% (Y)	
Australia	0.79		
Denmark	0.68		0.8%
Japan	0.60	0.7% (E)	
Sweden	0.59		
Iceland	0.47		
US	0.46	0.8%[6] (Y)	
Norway	0.45		
Italy	0.43		
Korea	(0.43)[5]	0.6% (E)	0.6%
Greece			0.4%
Ireland			0.3%

Note: In column (1), wastewater charges are excluded; the definition of "water charges" in column (2) varies slightly between countries; in columns (3) and (4), water charges are defined to include the provision of piped water supplies and the collection, treatment, and disposal of wastewater.
1.   Figure exceeds 3% "in many regions" in the low-income categories.
2.   Germany does not take part in the IWSA water bill survey. Similar calculations have therefore been undertaken, using the German average PWS charges figure per m^3 from the Ecologic study (1996-98). Although this figure is calculated in a manner consistent with the IWSA survey, it is still considered to be rather high, partly because the data available for use in the calculation are not strictly comparable.
3.   Figures range from 0.9% (Thames Water) to 1.9% (South West Water).
4.   Barcelona only (which has relatively high charges within Spain).
5.   As calculated by country experts.
6.   Figures for individual utilities ranged from 0.3% to 1.7% of median household incomes.
Sources: Col. (1) is calculated from data in IWSA (1997), as explained in the text.
     Col. (2) derived from country submissions to this study.
     Col. (3) from Ecotec (1996), Final Report, Table 5.12a.

Comparison of the Column 1 statistics with the current water prices (in US$) derived earlier (Table 13) demonstrates that:

  – Very low prices in international terms (*e.g.* **Hungary, Portugal,** and the **Czech Republic**) are sometimes associated with very high water supply charges, relative to *per capita* incomes (GDP).

– Countries with the highest water supply charges in international terms (*e.g.* **Denmark, France,** the **Netherlands, England and Wales,** and **Sweden**) do not necessarily reveal water charges that are the highest in relation to *per capita* incomes.

Column 2 reports the results of enquiries made for the present study on average water charges as a proportion of household incomes or expenditures. These percentages apply to all water charges, and are reassuringly consistent with the rankings indicated in Column 1. Column 3 presents similar statistics collected by Ecotec (1996) for its study of the application of the Polluter Pays Principle in **EU** Cohesion Fund countries (**Greece, Ireland, Portugal,** and **Spain**), and from other country submissions to this study. The years to which these data apply are unclear in the original report, which may explain some of the inconsistencies observed (*i.e.* for **Spain** and **Portugal**). What is most noticeable, however, are the relatively low figures for the four Cohesion Fund countries.

Chapter 11

Conclusions

11.1. Context and institutional change

There is some tendency for OECD water systems to be increasingly delivered by groupings of municipalities, in order to organise supply at a larger scale. This reflects a recognition that the provision of water services can be inefficient when too many independent water providers are involved in the process. The management autonomy enjoyed by local water utilities also seems to be increasing.

Broadly, the role of the national or regional government in water management is shifting from that of "primary service provider" to being the "creator and regulator" of the water supply system. In a small (but increasing) number of countries, independent economic regulators have been set up to regulate water prices on an autonomous basis. These economic regulators are usually in charge of setting prices, but may also have other responsibilities, such as establishing service performance standards.

Water supply regimes remain, on the whole, publicly owned, mainly because of the "natural monopoly" characteristics of these systems, which limit both the political and technical possibilities for introducing private markets into the management of water supplies. These limitations notwithstanding, an increasing number of countries are experimenting with various forms of private management of these regimes. A few countries have gone a considerable distance toward full privatisation of the water supply system.

Even where the water supply system remains publicly owned, *service management* is increasingly being delegated to private operators. This approach seems particularly well suited to decentralised systems, in which municipalities see delegation as a useful way of overcoming their own lack of technical expertise and/or financial resources. In several countries, service providers are permitted to decide whether they want to manage the service themselves (direct management), or to delegate management responsibility to a private operator ("concessions").

OECD 1999

11.2. Public water supply systems

Price structures

A wide range of price structures exist for water services in OECD countries. Even within individual countries or user groups, variations in charging systems can be significant. In the household sector, for example, water charging systems range from (conservation-oriented) increasing-block structures, to predominantly flat-fee systems (where there are few pressures to extend metering), to the completed abandonment of domestic water charges altogether.

Broadly, there is a trend away from fixed charges, and toward volumetric charging. Even where fixed charges persist, there is evidence of a shift toward the reduction (or even abolition) of large minimum free allowances.

Nevertheless, most countries still use two-part tariffs (*i.e.* with fixed and volumetric components) for their domestic water bills, with the volumetric portion making up 75 per cent or more of the total household water bill. Some countries already use 100 per cent volumetric pricing, and such a structure is under discussion in a few others. Within the volumetric part of the charge, there has been a shift in some countries away from decreasing-block tariffs, and toward increasing-block ones.

In the agricultural sector, the most common pricing structures are based on the surface area irrigated, and can be charged either at a flat-rate, or be differentiated according to crop type. Volume-based charges for irrigation water are the main charging systems used in at least five OECD countries. Other countries (or regions within countries) use either two-part tariffs, fixed prices, pumping charges, or average prices.

Where industrial users are supplied by public water systems, it appears that most are supplied out of the same system as household users, although a few countries have separate industrial networks. Typically, industrial users face the same pricing structures as household users do, although industrial users are virtually all metered, so volumetric pricing is more common in their case.

It is estimated that two-thirds of OECD household water consumption and almost 100 per cent of industrial consumption is now metered, and metering penetration continues to expand in most countries. Single-family houses are now 100 per cent metered in some countries. The situation in apartment blocks, where most of the population live, is more varied. Although the water supply entering apartment buildings is metered in nearly every OECD country, it is only in a few countries that separate metering is available for individual apartment residents.

Agricultural metering is less common, but some progress has been made in this direction recently in at least one country. In countries where water is relatively abundant, however, the costs of installing and reading meters on individual agricultural properties seems likely to exceed the efficiency benefits for the foreseeable future.

The expanded metering of water use is part of a general shift away from decreasing-block and flat-fee pricing structures, and toward uniform volumetric or increasing-block tariffs. While flat fees still dominate agricultural water pricing systems, some OECD countries have also been moving towards volumetric pricing systems in that sector as well. These shifts will eventually lead to the better reflection of marginal costs in water prices, and therefore to greater incentives for water conservation.

Some countries are seeking to refine their approach to marginal cost pricing by allowing for temporal variations in their water rate structures. The two most common variations of this approach include "within-the-day" variations in the household sector, and "seasonal" variations in rates applied to industry. However, both practices are still relatively new. Moreover, the absence of metering inhibits both the effectiveness and the efficiency of these alternative pricing strategies.

Metering the water use of individual consumers contributes significantly to the application of marginal cost pricing. This is because metering allows charging systems to be linked directly to individual consumption. Furthermore, as the real costs of water provision and disposal rise, the cost-benefit outlook for the metering decision becomes increasingly positive.

Table 33 attempts to categorise OECD countries according to the "strength of the conservation signal" generated by their current household water price structures.[25] For example, the presence of minimum charges and/or a significant fixed element in the water tariff will tend to "blunt" the conservation message, thereby lowering the strength of the signal. Predominantly flat-fee tariffs also act to reduce the signal's strength, while volumetric (particularly increasing-block volumetric) tariffs enhance it.

Price levels

Water prices in OECD countries have generally increased over the past ten years, and significantly so in a few countries. For example, in the household sector, of the 19 countries for which enough data was available to this study, all but one exhibited real per annum increases in water prices during this period. Five of these countries experienced average rates of price increase of 6 per cent or more per annum.

Data is not readily available for the agriculture sector, but it seems clear that price increases here are not occurring as quickly as they are in the household sector. Agriculture prices remain relatively low, as compared to households and industry, and a few countries actually apply no charges at all to irrigation water.

Because of the large quantities of water they use, industrial users are often able to negotiate special tariff structures and/or rates with the public utilities. Occasionally, these special arrangements deal with water quality variables, as well as quantity ones. Conversely, industrial users are occasionally subjected to extra charges related to "extra strength" pollutants.

Table 33. **Household Tariff** *Structures* **Categorised by Strength of the "Conservation Signal" (Late 1990s)**

Category	Countries Included	No. of Countries
"Cutting Edge" Conservation Pricing	Korea	1
Conservation or Social Pricing	Belgium, Greece, Japan, Italy, Mexico, Spain, Portugal, Turkey	8
Price times Quantity Volumetric	Czech Republic, Hungary, Poland	3
Traditional Volumetric	Austria, Denmark, Finland, France, Germany, Netherlands, Sweden, Switzerland	8
Mixed Volumetric	Australia, Luxembourg, US	3
Mixed (general)	Canada	1
Predominantly Flat-Fee	Iceland, New Zealand, Norway, UK	4
Domestic water charges consolidated into general taxation	Ireland	1
		29

11.3. Abstractions

Abstraction charges (charges for water used *outside of* the public supply system) are in place in at least 16 OECD countries, but are not usually found in countries where water is relatively abundant. Many of these charges have only recently been introduced. These charges tend to vary by the use to which the water is placed. While charges are most common for industrial direct abstractions, they are also found for agricultural water use and for direct abstractions by utilities supplying piped household water services.

In some countries, the abstraction charge has an explicit environmental objective, so the proceeds are allocated to an environmental fund. Abstraction charges directly related to the protection of groundwater exist in at least two countries.

11.4. Sewerage and sewage disposal

Increasing attention is being given in OECD countries to charging for wastewater disposal on the basis of treatment costs actually faced by service providers. For this reason, water charges related to pollution have increased substantially in recent years. Several countries are also increasing their water sewage charges with the explicit objective of generating sufficient revenues to fund new water treatment facilities. There is also a trend in the direction of separating treatment and supply charges on individual water bills – a step which will inevitably encourage more accountability on the part of service providers.

The pricing schemes in use for sewage-related services are not always clear, mainly because sewerage, sewage treatment, and drainage services are typically provided by different parts of the public service, each with its own principles and practices. However, sewage charges for households are generally directly related to volumes of water delivered from the public water supply system. Thus, the structure of wastewater charging systems tends to closely follow that of domestic water supply systems in most countries. This means that revenues for sewage services are based mainly on volumetric charges, usually in the context of a two-part (fixed and volumetric) arrangement.

The volume and characteristics of industrial sewage vary considerably from one company to another. Thus, industrial water consumption levels do not represent a good proxy for industrial sewerage and sewage disposal costs. As a result (and closely related to the shift toward more cost-reflective water tariffs for industry), there has been a trend towards the separate identification of sewerage and trade effluent prices for industrial sewage. The number of countries in which the costs of industrial sewage services are included in the price of water supply (or in general local taxes) has therefore been decreasing steadily.

Trade effluent charges are levied in 17 OECD countries, and are under consideration in a few others. Some municipalities do not use these charges because they are concerned about the competitiveness implications for local industry; others do not use them because they perceive the monitoring costs to be too high. Trade effluent charges usually depend on the metered volume of pollutants and/or pollution contents. In other cases, the charging formula can reflect the costs to the water treatment company of treating a particular effluent, or the "environmental sensitivity" of the receiving waters.

In countries where sewage service costs have risen significantly, industrial users have increasingly questioned whether the public sewer system represents the most cost-effective means of discharging their sewage. As a result, there is evidence of a trend toward more use of the self-treatment and effluent re-use options by industry.

Discharge controls are often imposed on direct sewage discharges (*i.e.* those which do not go through the public sewer). The most common form of discharge control is the need to have a permit to discharge directly back into the river or aquifer. Most OECD countries regulate the quality of waters into which discharges can be made, and breaking these quality standards usually leads to the imposition of fines.

11.5. Subsidies

In theory, "full cost recovery" should be a key policy objective whenever water infrastructure investments are made. Even where full cost recovery is not practised, transparency in the granting of any subsidies, either directly from general public revenues, or indirectly in the form of cross-subsidies from other user classes should be a "second best" policy objective.

In practice, it is still rare for OECD water infrastructure to be supplied on a "full cost recovery" basis. Despite generally (and sometimes rapidly) rising prices for water services in most countries, subsidies to water infrastructure are still common. Only a few countries currently base their household water pricing systems on the "full cost recovery" principle. On the other hand, there is a trend toward both lower levels of subsidy, and toward more public scrutiny in their design and delivery (transparency). The search for better cost recovery underlies many of the changes in OECD water laws and policies that have occurred in OECD countries over the past decade.

Because irrigated farming is often perceived as a means of promoting social and economic development objectives, water prices are often set in accordance with the (often *low*) profitability of each irrigated crop (or of the productivity of the land itself), rather than the actual costs of providing the water service. However, some of the more radical pricing reforms recently introduced in OECD countries are resulting in more emphasis being placed on making farmers responsible for the actual costs of their water demands.

As a result, several countries are making some progress toward the goal of full cost recovery for irrigation infrastructure. Nevertheless, only a small number of countries yet recover the full operating and maintenance costs of irrigation supply systems through charges, and none yet recover the full capital costs. In some cases, the shortfall is provided by government funds; in others there are cross-subsidies from water users in other sectors.

Full cost recovery is also gradually being implemented in the industrial sector, but subsidies to water use have never been as prevalent for industrial consumers as they have for other users. In particular, cross-subsidies from industrial users to farmers and households have long been characteristic of OECD water pricing policies. These cross-subsidies are increasingly being recognised, and are gradually being reduced.

The principle of "full cost recovery" is being increasingly applied to the pricing of sewage services, as it is to the provision of water supply services. However, it is apparent that a considerable backlog of investment needs exists in wastewater treatment capacity in several OECD countries. In these cases, full recovery via user charges of capital costs seems unlikely over the near-term.

11.6. Effects of pricing on water demand

Although water consumption has been generally increasing over the last decade in many OECD countries, it has also been reduced or held stable in several others. The area of agricultural land that is irrigated, for example, seems to have largely stabilised. Industrial demands, on the other hand, have generally decreased in OECD countries, partly because of general shifts from industrial to service-based economies, and partly because of increased efficiencies in water use.

Most studies indicate that, in aggregate, households, businesses and agricultural producers *do* change their water consumption patterns in response to changes in such variables as price levels, metering penetration, and seasonal pricing. In some cases, response rates can be quite high, especially for higher-income households.

Some individual branches of industry (*e.g.* chemicals, pulp and paper, textiles, and metallurgy) have also made significant progress in reducing their water demands in recent years. One reason for these decreases is that these particular industrial sectors appear to be relatively sensitive to changes in water prices, reflecting their ability to make use of new water-saving technologies in their production processes, as these become available.

For agricultural users, higher price levels in the long run can lead to the adoption of more efficient irrigation technologies; to improvements in on-farm water management practices; and (perhaps) to reductions in the amount of land being irrigated. Where prices can be reformed to better reflect the full economic costs of irrigation water supply (and, if possible, the environmental effects as well), available evidence suggests that water conservation may be improved in some cases.

11.7. Social objectives

Access to the public water system is no longer a serious problem in most OECD countries, with at least 75 per cent of the population (and often as high as 90 per cent) already being serviced. Those countries with large rural populations are typically the ones with the lowest service access rates.

Although access rates are high, significant concerns about the affordability of water still remain. A few countries have therefore developed (or are currently discussing) innovative tariff designs to address these social concerns.

Broadly, countries approach the problem of injecting social considerations into water prices either from the perspective of the tariff structure (tariff-based solutions) or from the perspective of the particular group of water user involved (target-group solutions).

For example, the "social progressivity" of increasing-block tariffs is often stressed as a way of making the tariff system less onerous on lower-income users. The observed shifts in the direction of increasing-block structures can therefore be attributed partly to social goals. (Note, however, that this shift also encourages water conservation – an environmental goal – in addition to being consistent with marginal cost pricing – an economic objective.)

There is a growing awareness in OECD countries that: *i*) subsidising water use is not necessarily the best way to achieve sectoral economic or social objectives and *ii*) some economic and social goals are actually harmed over the longer-term by using a subsidy-based approach. General reductions in water prices shield all consumers (*i.e.* not just those in need of assistance) from important economic and environmental signals. Because of this, several OECD countries have been experimenting with their water price regimes, so as to better "target" those groups most in need of assistance.

Notes

1. Abstractions consist of total water withdrawals, regardless of amounts later returned to the watercourse.
2. In general, however, statistics of water use for power purposes mainly refers to cooling purposes, and hydro-power (turbine) water is usually *not* included.
3. This includes freshwater abstractions from both surface and groundwater.
4. Occasionally, this may have a negative effect on water conservation, in that the savings obtained from the use of new technologies may actually make it profitable to utilise *more* water.
5. This is sometimes referred to as "historic" financial obligations. Recent developments in inflation accounting have led to moves towards charges providing for depreciation based on "current costs", as well as covering the opportunity cost of public sector capital ("economic" financial obligations) (OECD, 1987*a*).
6. Empresas Portuguesa das Aguas Livres (EPAL) has been responsible for water services in Lisbon since 1867.
7. In such cases, it might be appropriate to look for proxies for the contribution a user should make to peak costs, such as the maximum flow of the consumer's supply pipe per unit period of time. The fixed charge could thus be geared to the potential peak demand that a consumer may make on the system. However, under such circumstances, the fixed charge provides no incentive to reduce peak demands.
8. A private company supplying water to its clients would be more likely to take this view than, say, a municipal utility, which may be more likely to pursue equity as one of its objectives.
9. These trials are unlikely to take place before the year 2000, and then only on a voluntary basis.
10. There have been trials in England, however, with time-of-day tariff variations for domestic water use. See Box 14.
11. The framework was applied to the eight countries for which the data availability was deemed to be most suitable: **Canada, Germany, Mexico,** the **Netherlands, Poland, Portugal,** the **UK,** and the **US.** See OECD (1999*a*) for a detailed description of the methodology that was used.
12. The consumption level corresponding to each type of user varies slightly from country to country, according to the data availability in each country.
13. Of course, some of these "supply" attributes are highly correlated with costs incurred in providing the water service in the first place. But this correlation becomes blurred when one looks in more detail at how water use for irrigation has historically evolved in a given basin or catchment area. For example, "first-comers" tend to enjoy cheaper and more convenient access to water than "late-comers" do.

14. This applies only to those rivers whose flows are "supported" by releases from reservoirs by other activities managed by the Environment Agency.

15. Ninety-six per cent of wastewater charges are derived from non-volumetric elements in *Australia.*

16. In the **Netherlands,** state waters (large bodies of water of national importance, such as the river Rhine and river Meuse and lake Ijssel) are managed by the central government and other bodies of surface water of lesser importance are the responsibility of the provinces or, by delegation, of the (regional) Water Boards.

17. The only exceptions are a few small municipalities where it is used to eliminate a heavy social impact on household water users.

18. It is reported that this shortfall originated from ineffective levying of the water abstraction charges.

19. These shortcomings did not originate from the "underpricing" of water services, but from administrative difficulties in collecting the charges that ought to be paid.

20. It should also be noted that the more sophisticated panel data techniques reflected in this set of estimates give values of the same order of magnitude as those generated by conventional models.

21. Although this depends on the width of the blocks and the steepness of the rise of the rate in the increasing-block structure.

22. The standard household examined constitutes two adults and two children, using 200 m^3 of potable water per annum (therefore, an average of 137 lhd), and living in a single family house with certain characteristics defined in order to specify the charges required by some local utilities (lot size, number of rooms, number of taps, etc. (see Achtienribbe Homer, Papp and Wiederkehr (1992) for further details).

23. No account is taken of wastewater charges in the IWSA surveys, unlike the data for the other columns of this table.

24. The resulting quotients have been multiplied by 100 for ease of interpretation.

25. This table is based purely on price *structures*, and does not take account of price *levels*. In particular, it takes no account of the extent to which subsidisation in any given country may be preventing the economic and environmental costs from being reflected in water charges.

Full Cost Recovery

Table A1 below offers one way of classifying costs for household water usage, together with the various charges, taxes and levies which may appear separately on a water bill (OECD, 1999c). Some of these taxes (*e.g.* VAT) may occasionally be "justified" as a way of recovering some of the environmental costs that are incurred. In other instances, they may be presented as a method of raising general government revenues (*e.g.* as part of a general VAT rate, levied on a whole range of goods and services).

Using the taxonomy shown in Table A1, "full cost recovery" can be defined in two ways. First, if T_p and T_w are seen as contributing to general revenues, and no cross-subsidisation between different water services takes place, the FCR requirement is "strong", and can be defined as:

$$C_p + S_p \geq O_p + K_p + A_a + A_c + A_d$$
$$and \quad C_w + S_w \geq O_w + K_w + P_a + P_c + P_d.$$

Table A1. **Cost and Revenue Classification for "Full Cost Recovery" Measurement**

		Public Water Supply		Wastewater	
Costs					
1.	Direct Economic Costs	Operating Expenditures (Opex)	O_p	Opex	O_w
		Capital Expenditures (Capex)	K_p	Capex	K_w
2.	Related Environmental Costs	Abstraction Licence Fees (administration)	A_a	Pollution Licence Fees (administration)	P_a
		Abstraction Charges	A_c	Pollution Charges	P_c
		Scarcity Costs/Rents	A_s	Additional Pollution Damage (losses to producers or consumers)	P_d
		Additional Abstractions Costs: Damages	A_d		
Revenues					
1.	Charges/Tariffs		C_p		C_w
2.	Specific Taxes	On water use	S_p	On wastewater	S_w
3.	General Taxes (VAT, etc.)	On PWS	T_p	On wastewater	T_w

Note: Because Table A1 is only intended to help conceptualise "full cost recovery", there is no need to be precise about how the various costs and revenues should be measured. It may be helpful, however, to imagine all costs and revenues on an annual basis: any one-off costs (*e.g.* investments) and revenues (*e.g.* connection fees) would then be viewed as "annual equivalents". Although A_s is a cost that may be charged, it does not constitute a factor input reward, and thus does not need to be recovered in aggregate. The avoidance of pure "supernormal" profits may be achieved through the use of multi-part tariffs.

In the second scenario, however, the general taxes (T_p and T_w) are "permitted" to have a role in cost-recovery, such that the FCR requirement is "weak", and may be stated as:

$$C_p + S_p + T_p \geq O_p + K_p + A_a + A_c + A_d$$
$$and \quad C_w + S_w + T_w \geq O_w + K_w + P_a + P_c + P_d.$$

Because of serious difficulties in placing a monetary evaluation on environmental costs many of these costs cannot easily be included in practice in the establishment of water charges. In principle, however, FCR requires that all such costs be taken into account.

The absence of full cost-recovery in a water charging system generally means either that subsidies are in place to make up the difference between costs and the water charges (so that the water utility can be financially sustainable), or that the asset base is being run-down. As such, FCR has an environmental cost dimension, insofar as it may encourage the sustainable use of water resources over time.

References

ACHTIENRIBBE, G., V. HOMER, E. PAPP and W. WIEDERKWEHR (1992),
"International Comparison of Drinking Water Prices", *Aqua*, Vol. 41, No. 6, pp. 360-363.

ANDERSEN, M.S. (1996),
Water Supply and Water Prices in Denmark, Aarhus Centre for Social Science Research on the Environment/Aarhus University.

ANON (1992),
"Canadian Water Utility Makes Successful Switch to Metering", *Water Engineering and Management*, Vol. 139, March, pp. 20-26.

ANON (1993),
"Water Meters at Work: System-Wide Metering Helps Solve Shortage Problems", *Water Engineering and Management*, Vol. 140, No. 6, p. 31.

BARRAQUE, B. and S. CAMBON (1997),
"Appendix B: France", in *Water Research Centre* (1997), *op. cit.*

BARRETT, A., J. LAWLOR and S. SCOTT (1997),
The Fiscal System and the Polluter Pays Principle, Ashgate, Avebury, Aldershot, Hampshire.

BATIE, S. (1997),
"Environmental Benefits of Agriculture: Non-European OECD Countries", in OECD, *Environmental Benefits from Agriculture: Issues and Policies*, OECD, Paris.

BEECHER, J.A. (1994),
"Water Affordability and Alternatives to Service Disconnection", *Journal of the American Water Works Association*, Vol. 86, No. 10, pp. 61-65.

BEECHER, J.A. and P.C. MANN (1997),
"Real Water Rates on the Rise", *Public Utilities Fortnightly*, Vol. 135, No. 14, pp. 42-46.

BRAGANÇA, J. (1998),
Personal communication, Portugal.

BRILL, E., E. HOCHMAN and D. ZILBERMAN (1997),
"Allocating and Pricing at the Water District Level", *American Journal of Agricultural Economics* 79(4), pp. 952-963.

CAMBON-GRAU, S. and B. BARRAQUÉ (1996),
"Comparing Water Prices in Europe – France", in ECOLOGIC (1996-98), *op. cit.*

CAMBON-GRAU, S. and J.M. BERLAND (1998),
"Sewerage Charges in France", in ECOLOGIC (1997-98), *op. cit.*

CASTRO CALDAS, J. (1997),
"Portugal", in *Water Pricing Experiences. An International Perspective* (eds. A. Dinar and A. Subramanian), World Bank Technical Paper No. 386, Washington DC, pp. 99-103.

165|

CHICOINE, D.L. and G. RAMAMURTHY (1986),
"Evidence on the Specification of Price in the Study of Domestic Water Demand". Land Economics, Vol. 62, No. 1, pp. 26-32.

CHICOINE, D.L., S.C. DELLER and G. RAMAMURTHY (1986),
"Water Demand Estimation Under Block Rate Pricing: A Simultaneous Equation Approach", Water Resources Research, Vol. 22, No. 6, pp. 859-863.

COMMONWEALTH OF AUSTRALIA (1996),
Subsidies to the Use of Natural Resources: Water,
http://www.erin.gov.au/portfolio/dest/subs/subs8.htm, 12 August 1996.

CONSO 2000 (1996),
EAU: Résultats de l'enquête, CONSO 2000, mimeo.

CORREIA, F.N. et al. (1997),
"Portugal", in Institutionen der Wasserwirtschaft in Europa, Berlin, Springer, pp. 479-581.

CRITELLI, A. (1998),
"Elasticity Estimate Calculated from Equations", Personal Communication from A. Massarutto, Universita di Udine, May.

DESTRO, S. (1997),
"Italy", In DINAR and SUBRAMANIAN (eds.), op. cit.

DIETZ, C. and J. RANTON (1995),
"Targetted Programming for Low-income Households", Paper 10C-3, presented to Conser 96 Conference, American Water Works Association, Denver.

DINAR, A. and A. SUBRAMANIAN (1997),
Water Pricing Experiences. An International Perspective, World Bank Technical Paper No. 386, Washington DC.

DINAR, A. and D. ZILBERMAN (eds.) (1991),
The Economics and Management of Water and Drainage in Agriculture, Kluwer A.P., Norwell, Massachusetts.

DOE (DEPARTMENT OF THE ENVIRONMENT) (1993),
Water Metering Trials: Final Report, Department of the Environment, London.

DUCHEIN A. (1997),
"France: Partnership between the Agricultural Community and the Basin Agencies", in OECD (1998c), op. cit.

DUKE, E.M. and A.C. MONTOYA (1993),
"Trends in Water Pricing: Results of Ernst and Young's National Rate Surveys", Journal of the American Water Works Association, Vol. 85, No. 5, pp. 55-61.

ECOLOGIC (1996-98),
Country Case Studies on Water Pricing and English Summary, report prepared for UFOPLAN Research Plan 102/04/427, on contract to the German Federal Environment Agency, Berlin, various mimeo reports.

ECOLOGIC (1997-98),
Country Case Studies on Sewerage Pricing, report prepared on contract to the German Federal Environment Agency, Berlin, various mimeo reports.

ECOTEC (1996),
The Application of the Polluter Pays Principle in Cohesion Fund Countries (Annexes 1 to 4), Ecotec Research and Consulting Limited, Birmingham and Brussels.

EDWARDS, K. (1996),
"The Role of Leakage Control and Metering in Effective Demand Management", paper delivered at *Conference on Water 96: Investing in the Future*, London.

EIDGENÖSSISCHES DEPARTEMENT DES INNERN (1996),
Änderung des Gewässerschutzgesetzes. Nachhaltige Finanzierung der Abwasser- und Abfallentsorgung (Einführung des Verursacherprinzips und weiterer Abbau der Subventionen).

ENVIRONMENT AGENCY (1996),
Water Conservation Planning: USA Case Studies Project Final Report, Amy Vickers and Associates, Inc., Boston.

EUROSTAT (1997),
Water Prices in the 15 Member States of the EU, Pilot Study of Luxembourg, Joint Eurostat/EFTA Sub-Group on Water Statistics, Statistical Office of the European Communities.

FEDERICO, K. (1990),
"Experience in Mandating Water Conservation Pricing in Palm Beach County", in BLOOME, M.W. (ed.), *Rate Structures to Promote Conservation: Conference Proceedings*, Delaware River Basin Commission and New York City Waterboard.

FEVRIER, P. (1999),
Personal Communication, France (25 March).

FOX, T.P. (1995),
"Analysis, Design and Implementation of a Conservation Rate Structure", paper 2F-1 delivered at *Conserve 96* Conference, American Water Works Association, Denver.

GAO (1996),
Bureau of Reclamation: Information on Allocation and Repayment of Costs of Constructing and Operating Water Projects, report to the Ranking Minority Member, Committee on Resources, House of Representatives (GAO/RCED-96-109), United States General Accounting Office, Washington DC.

GARDNER, B.D. (1997),
"Some Implications of Federal Grazing, Timber, Irrigation, and Recreation Subsidies", *Choices*, Third Quarter, pp. 9-14.

GRIEG, J. (1997),
"Some Practical Perspectives on Water Pricing Reform From an Agricultural Viewpoint", in OECD (1998c), *op. cit.*

HANSEN, L.G. (1996),
"Water and Energy Price Impacts on Residential Water demand in Copenhagen", *Land Economics*, Vol. 72, No. 1, pp. 66-79.

HARDEN, B. (1996),
A River Lost: The Life and Death of the Columbia, New York, London, W.W. Norton and Company.

HERRINGTON, P.R. (1997a),
"Pricing Water Properly", in O'RIORDAN (1997), *Ecotaxation*, Earthscan, London.

HERRINGTON, P.R. (1997b),
"Long-Run Marginal Cost Estimates in the Public Water Supply in England and Wales", Appendix C in HILLS, B., M. HUBY and P. KENWAY, *Fair and Sustainable: Paying for Water*, New Policy Institute, London.

167

HOGLUND, L. (1997),
"Estimation of Household Demand for Water in Sweden and its Implications for a Potential Tax on Water Use", *Studies in Environmental Economics and Development*, 1997:12 Department of Economics, Gothenburg University, Gothenburg.

HORBULYK, T.M. and L.J. LO. (1998),
"Potential Water Markets in Alberta, Canada", in EASTER, K.W., M. ROSEGRANT and A. DINAR (eds.), *Markets for Water* – Potential and Performance, Kluwer Academic Publishers, New York, in press.

IWSA (INTERNATIONAL WATER SUPPLY ASSOCIATION) (1988),
International Water Statistics, IWSA, Zurich.

IWSA (INTERNATIONAL WATER SUPPLY ASSOCIATION) (1997),
International Statistics for Water Supply, IWSA, Vienna.

JOHNSON III, S.H. (1997),
"Irrigation Management Transfer: Decentralising Public Irrigation in Mexico", *Water International* 22, pp. 159-167.

KAY, S. (1998),
Personal Communication, 20 February.

KIM, T.Y. (1998),
"Water Pricing Policy for the Optimal Management of Water Resources" (in Korean).

KOPLOW, D., E. CLARK, *et al.* (1996),
Improving Industrial Pretreatment: Success Factors, Challenges, and Project Ideas. Findings from EPA Site Visits to California, Indiana and Virginia. October 1996, Cambridge, Massachusetts: Industrial Economics Incorporated.

KPMG (1996),
Financing of Local Government in Ireland, report prepared by KPMG Consultants for the Irish Department of the Environment.

KRAEMER, R.A. and H. NOWELL-SMITH (1997),
"Appendix C: Germany", in *Water Research Centre* (1997), *op. cit.*

KRAGH, P. (1998),
"Sewerage Charges and the Cost of Sewerage Services in Denmark", in ECOLOGIC (1997-98), *op. cit.*

LAW, G.R. (1986),
"Water Use in Urban Auckland, New Zealand", paper presented to the *National Workshop of the American Water Works Association*, Vol. 74, No. 6.

LEKAKIS, J. (1998),
Personal Communication, Greece.

LIPPIATT, B.C. and S.F. WEBER (1982),
"Water Rates and Residential Water Conservation", *Journal of the American Water Works Association*, Vol. 74, No. 6.

MAESTU, J. (1996),
Comparing Water Prices in Europe: The Case of Spain (Working Title), Draft report for Ecologic and the German Ministry for Enviroment.

MANIATI-SIATOU (1998),
Personal Communication (16 October), Hellenic Republic Ministry of Development, Directorate of Water and Natural Resources, Athens.

MARKUS, E. (1993),
Personal Communication (3 February), Ernst and Young, New York.

MASSARUTTO, A. (1993),
Economia del ciclo dell'acqua, Milanon, FrancoAngeli.

MASSARUTTO, A. (1996),
Comparing Water Prices in Europe: Water Prices in Italy, Final draft report for Ecologic and the German Ministry for Enviroment, IEFE, Bocconi University, Milano.

MASSARUTTO, A. (1999),
Personal Communication (12 March), Dipartimento di Scienze Economiche, Università di Udine, Spain.

MASSARUTTO, A. and L. MESSORI (1998),
"Sewerage Charges in Italy", in ECOLOGIC (1997-98), op. cit.

MAYOR'S BLUE RIBBON COMMITTEE ON WATER RATES (1992),
City of Los Angeles – Proposed Water Rates, Mayor's Blue Ribbon Committee, Los Angeles.

MID-KENT (1997),
Meter Pilot Project Report 1, Mid-Kent Water PLC, Snodland, UK.

MINISTÈRE DE L'ÉCONOMIE ET DES FINANCES (1996),
Enquête sur le prix de l'eau 1991-1996, Service Public 2000, Paris.

MONTGINOUL, M. and T. RIEU (1996),
"Instruments économiques et gestion de l'eau d'irrigation en France", La Houille Blanche 8, pp. 47-54.

MONTGINOUL, M. and T. RIEU (1996),
"Instruments de gestion de l'eau d'irrigation en France : exemple de la Charente", Ingénieries-EAT 8, pp. 3-12.

NAKASHIMA, Y.J. (1997),
"The Japanese Experience with Sustainable Water Use in Agriculture: Existing Systems and the Possibility of Introducing Market Mechanisms", in OECD (1998c), op. cit.

NAUGES, C. and A. THOMAS (1998),
"Efficient Estimation of Residential Water Demand with Panel Data", paper presented at EAERE Annual Meeting, Venice, June, Université des Sciences Sociales de Toulouse, Toulouse.

NIESWIADOMY, M.L. and D.J. MOLINA (1989),
"Comparing Residential Water Demand Estimates Under Decreasing and Increasing-block Rates Using Household Data", Land Economics, Vol. 65, No. 3, pp. 281-289.

NYS, R. (1998),
Personal Communication, Vlaamse Maatschappij Voor Watervoorziening, Belgium.

NYS, R. (1999),
"The Free Allowance in the Flanders Region", paper presented at "L'Europe de l'eau, l'eau des Européens : la place des outils économiques", Lille (9-10 February).

OECD (1987a),
Pricing of Water Services, OECD, Paris.

OECD (1987b),
Improved Water Demand Management: State of the Art Report, Document ENV/NRM/87.2/REV1, OECD, Paris.

OECD (1989),
   Water Resource Management: Integrated Policies, OECD, Paris.

OECD (1991),
   Environmental Policy: How to Apply Economic Instruments, OECD, Paris.

OECD (1996),
   Implementation Strategies for Environmental Taxes, OECD, Paris.

OECD (1997),
   Water Subsidies and the Environment, Document OCDE/GD(97)220, OECD, Paris.

OECD (1998a),
   Towards Sustainable Development: Environmental Indicators, OECD, Paris.

OECD (1998b),
   Improving the Environment through Reducing Subsidies, OECD, Paris.

OECD (1998c),
   Sustainable Management of Water in Agriculture, OECD, Paris.

OECD (1998d),
   Water Management: Performances and Challenges, OECD, Paris.

OECD (1999a),
   Industrial Water Pricing in OECD Countries, Document ENV/EPOC/GEEI(98)10/FINAL, OECD, Paris.

OECD (1999b),
   Agricultural Water Pricing in OECD Countries, Document ENV/EPOC/GEEI(98)11/FINAL, OECD, Paris.

OECD (1999c),
   Household Water Pricing in OECD Countries, Document ENV/EPOC/GEEI(98)12/FINAL, OECD, Paris.

OFFICE OF WATER SERVICES (1998),
   1998-99 *Report on Tariff Structure and Charges*. Office of Water Services, Birmingham.

OLMSTEAD, J., D. SUNDING, D. PARKER, R. HOWITT and D. ZILBERMAN (1997),
   "Water Marketing in The '90s: Entering the Electronic age", *Choices*, Third Quarter, pp. 15-19.

PÉREZ-DIAZ, V., J. MEZO and B. ÁLVAREZ-MIRANDA (1996),
   Política y economía del agua en España, Círculo de Empresarios, Madrid.

PAVLÍK, S. (1996),
   Information on Subsidies in Water Supply, Sewerage, and in Agriculture, Czech Republic, manuscript.

PEZZEY, J.C.V. and G.A. MILL (1998),
   A Review of Tariffs for Public Water Supply, A Report to the Environment Agency, National Water Demand Management Centre, Worthing, West Sussex.

POINT, P. (1993),
   "Partage de la ressource en eau et demande d'alimentation en eau potable", *Revue Économique*, 4, pp. 849-862.

RAFTELIS ENVIRONMENTAL CONSULTING GROUP, INC. (1998),
   Water and Wastewater Rate Survey?, Raftelis Environmental Consulting Group, Inc., Charlotte, North Carolina.

RAFTELIS, G.A. (1989),
  The Arthur Young Guide to Water and Wastewater Finance and Pricing, Lewis Publishers, Chelsea, Michigan.

RAINELLI, P. and D. VERMERSCH (1998),
  Irrigation in France: Current Situation and Reasons for its Development, unpublished manuscript from a study submitted to OECD Environment Directorate.

RASKIN, P.D., E. HANSEN and R.M. MARGOLIS (1996),
  "Water and Sustainability: Global Patterns and Long-range Problems", *Natural Resources Forum* 20, (1), pp. 1-17.

RECH, T. (1998),
  Personal Communication, Austria.

REDAUD, J.L. (1997),
  "Indicators to Measure the Impact of Agriculture on Water Use Pricing and Cost of Water Services", in OECD (1998b), *op. cit.*

REES, J. (1997),
  "United Kingdom", in DINAR and SUBRAMANIAN (eds.), *op. cit.*

RENWICK, M. and S. ARCHIBALD (1997),
  "Demand-Side Management Policies for Residential Water Use: Who Bears the Conservation Burden?", University of Minnesota.

ROSEBERG, P. (1994),
  Water and Wastewater International, February.

SANCLEMENTE (undated),
  Influence of Metering on Water Consumption.

SCHAFTER, J.E. and E.L. DAVID (1985),
  "Estimating Residential Water Demand Under Multi-Part Tariffs Using Aggregate Data", *Land Economics*, Vol. 61, No. 3, pp. 272-280.

SCHAILBLE, G.D. (1997),
  "Water Conservation Policy Analysis: An Interregional, Multi-Output, Primal-Dual Optimization Approach", *American Journal of Agricultural Economics*, 79(1), pp. 163-177.

SELIANITIS, P. (1997),
  "Greece: Sustainable Management of Water in Agriculture: Issues and Policies", in OECD (1998b), *op. cit.*

SJOHOLT, K.E. (1996),
  Water Subsidies and their Environmental Implications, Norway, manuscript.

SMETS, H. (forthcoming 1999),
  "Le principe utilisateur-payeur pour la gestion durable des ressources naturelles", mimeo.

STEVENS, T.H., J. MILLER and C. WILLIS (1992),
  "Effect of Price Structure on Residential Water Demand", *Water Resources Bulletin*, Vol. 28, No. 4, pp. 681-685.

SUMPSI, J.M., A. GARRIDO, M. BLANCO, C. VARELA, E. IGLESIAS and L. AVELLÁ (1996),
  Estudio sobre la economía del agua y la competitividad de los regadíos españoles, Informe Final para la Secretaría General de Desarrollo Rural y Defensa de la Naturaleza, MAPA, Madrid.

SYDNEY WATER (1998),
   Submission to the Independent Pricing and Regulatory Tribunal of New South Wales Review of 1996 Medium Term Price Path Determination for Sydney Water Corporation, Sydney Water Corporation, Sydney.

TATE D.M. and D.N. SCHARF (1995),
   "Water Use in Canadian Industry, 1991", *Social Science Series*, No.31, Water and Habitat Conservation Branch, Ottawa, Canada.

TATE, D.M. and D.M. LACELLE (1995),
   Municipal Water Rates in Canada: Current Practices and Prices, 1991, report for the Water and Habitat Conservation Branch, Canadian Wildlife Service, Environment Canada, Ottawa.

TATE, D.N. and R. RIVERS (1990),
   "Industrial Water Pricing for Ontario: Towards Realistic Pricing", in *International and Transboundary Water Resources Issues: American Water and Resources Association* (April), pp. 463-472.

TSUR, Y. and A. DINAR (1997),
   "The Relative Efficiency and Implementation Costs of Alternative Methods for Pricing Irrigation Water", *The World Bank Economic Review*, 11(2), pp. 243-62.

UNIDO (1996a),
   "Industry and Water: Options for Management and Conservation – Technical Report: Findings and Recommendations", unpublished document.

UNITED NATIONS (1992),
   Rio Declaration on Environment and Development, report of the United Nations Confence on Environment and Development, Rio de Janeiro (3-14 June).

UNITED NATIONS (1997a),
   Programme for the Further Implementation of Agenda 21 (S/19-2), Resolution adopted by the General Assembly at its nineteenth special session, 19 September.

UNITED NATIONS (1997b),
   Comprehensive Assessment of the Freshwater Resources of the World (E/CN.17/1997/9), Commission on Sustainable Development, Fifth Session, 7-25 April.

VAN DEN BERGEN, V.W.J. (1993),
   Funding the Water Cycle in the Netherlands, Proceedings of a Workshop on Economic and Financial Instruments in Environmental Policy (Warsaw).

WAHL, R. (1989),
   Markets for Federal Water: Subsidies, Property Rights, and the US Bureau of Reclamation, Resources for the Future, Washington DC.

WAHL, R.W. (1989),
   Markets for Federal Water: Subsidies, Property Rights, and the Bureau of Reclamation, Washington DC, Resources for the Future.

WALLACH, T. (1996),
   Information Regarding Water and Wastewater, Denmark. manuscript.

WARNER, R. (1995),
   Water Pricing and the Marginal Cost of Water, Sydney Water Corporation, Sydney.

WATER RESEARCH CENTRE (1994),
   The Effects of Metered Charging on Customer Demand for Water from 1 April 1989 to 31 March 1993, Report UC 2072, Water Research Centre, Swindon.

WELSH, C. (1991),

"A Contingent Valuation Study of Consumers' Willingness to Pay for Water: An Approach to Conserving Christchurch's Groundwater Resource", Thesis submitted for M.Sc. degree, Lincoln University.

WILCHENS, D. (1991),

"Increasing Block-rate Prices for Irrigation Water Motivate Drain Water Reduction", in DINAR and ZILBERMAN, *op. cit.*

ZABEL, T.F. and N. ORMAN (1996),

Water Prices in Europe – UK (England and Wales), Case Study by the Water Research Centre (WRC).